What a Difference a Team Makes

Hugh Steven

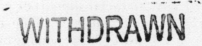

What a Difference a Team Makes

Hugh Steven

CREDO
PUBLISHING CORPORATION

Canadian Cataloguing in Publication Data

Steven, Hugh.
What a difference a team makes

ISBN 0-920479-24-3

1. Wycliffe Associates - History.
2. Bible - Translating - History. I. Title.
BV2370.W94S84 1988   266'.006'01   C88-091246-4

Published by CREDO Publishing Corporation
All Rights Reserved

ISBN 0-920479-24-3
(paperback)

Cover by Randy Watson

CREDO Publishing Corporation
17919 Roan Place
Cloverdale, British Columbia V3S 5K1

Printed in the United States of America

Acknowledgments

In the general scheme of book writing, it's generally easier for me to begin a book than end it. This was particularly true for this volume. The deeper I dug into the records, the richer became the vein of people's experiences. While each experience of *how* they became involved with Wycliffe Associates was unique, the *why* was most often the same. Each wanted to be part of a team, to be part of an experience that would make a difference in the world and bring glory to the name of Jesus Christ while advancing the cause of Bible translation. I here thank all who have given of themselves and their time and money to the ongoing ministry of Wycliffe Bible translators and Wycliffe Associates.

My thanks to longtime friend and colleague, Mary Cates, for her wonderful sense of WA's corporate history, and for her skill as a copy editor and photo archivist. Dr. Dale W. Keitzman, also a longtime friend and colleague, is due an equal word of thanks for his keen historical memory and for the courage to push ahead on his initial vision for WA. Also to Bill Butler who shared the vision and demonstrated true Christian love and faith with concrete action. To Jim Hefley, my friend and onetime mentor, for the use of some selected materials that appeared in his earlier book on WA,

God's Freelancers. John Bender is due a word of appreciation for his helpful suggestions on the construction ministry. My thanks to Kim Beaty who took time away from her own writing schedule and preparation for an overseas trip to assist me with several important and lengthy interviews. Special thanks to Ken Harris and John Hamilton for their artistic input on the cover design.

I also want to thank Roger Tompkins, who filled in as Acting President of WA (a position he held on an earlier occasion), for his willingness to assume yet another administrative responsibility until the election of WA's new president, Martin Huyett, in May 1988.

A special word of thanks to my part-time secretary, Valarie Sluss, for her speedy and efficient keyboarding of this manuscript. Also to Ruth O. Larssen for her help in proofreading and copyediting, a skill she learned while working at WA. And to my wife Norma who quietly works behind the scenes as editor and full colleague in our joint writing ministry. I most assuredly could not write without her help and encouragement.

Finally, a special word of appreciation to Al Ginty. As this book goes to press, Al has relinquished his role as WA's president. I here thank him for his friendship to me and to Wycliffe books.

Introduction

"Blessed to Be a Blessing"

> Christians are Christ's body, the organism
> through which He works. Every addition to that
> body enables Him to do more.   —C.S. Lewis

Like Wycliffe Bible Translators (WBT) and the
Summer Institute of Linguistics (SIL), Wycliffe Associates (WA) began with an idea. "And," said the late Joe
Bayly, "all good ideas are a gift from God." Yet, ideas,
no matter how good, must be acted upon if they are to
make a difference in the course of history.

In 1918, a year after William Cameron Townsend,
founder of Wycliffe Bible Translators, began his ministry
as a colporteur in Guatamala,† he became captive to
a series of principles or ideas that would guide him and
the worldwide organizations he would one day found.
His ideas then, of course, were unformulated. He had
no special technique or organization to give them
shape. Nor did he, at that time, envision how important
his ideas would become. He hadn't the slightest inkling
that one day, in the providence of God, he would

---

† See *A Thousand Trails,* Personal Journal of William Cameron
Townsend, 1917-1918, edited and compiled by Hugh Steven, Credo
Publishers. Available through the WBT Bookroom.

become one of the world's foremost mission statesmen.

In May 1918, Mr. Townsend wrote a letter to his parents and younger brother Paul, then living in Southern California. Just eight months had passed since he and his friend Robbie Robertson had set sail from San Francisco for Guatemala. But they had been eight months of high adventure as he galvanized his priorities and allowed the Holy Spirit to bring into focus the vision God had planned for him: that he be actively involved in the Church's mission.

By "mission" he understood he was to minister to the spiritual and physical needs of Guatemala's ethnic peoples, specifically the Cakchiquels. "The desire to start a school," he wrote, "grows like a fire every day. I think a school that would teach reading, writing and arithemetic, together with agriculture and various trades such as carpentry, shoemaking and, of course, the Bible, would be an unequaled force in evangelizing the Indians of Central America."

In previous letters and those that followed, Mr. Townsend outlined several grand possibilities of how his parents, then in their early seventies, and younger brother Paul, a carpenter and handyman, could become involved in extending the kingdom of God through their practical skills and talents.

Tempered by almost a year's experience in Guatemala, the principle that emerged from his youthful energy was that it takes all kinds of people, with all kinds of talents and gifts to fulfill the mandate of the Great Commission. He learned early that Bible translation is a specialized talent, as is carpentry, bookkeeping, teaching, writing, driving a truck or supervising a children's home or group dining room.

Mr. Townsend never allowed the notion to develop that a linguist or Bible translator or so-called "full-time" missionary belonged to an ascetic elite. Obedience to God meant obedience to the imperatives of mission. Thus no one was exempt. In Mr. Townsend's mind, worldwide evangelism was the central task of the Church, and every Christian was a missionary. His hope was that all would become involved, in one way or another, in the great cause of reaching the world's ethnic minorities with the Good News of Jesus Christ.

Since its beginning in June 1967, Wycliffe Associates, the official lay support organization of Wycliffe Bible Translators, has endeavored to implement Mr. Townsend's early principle. Through the provision of a variety of service options, they have involved hundreds of lay people in the Bible translation ministry. They have also adopted another of Mr. Townsend's principles. It's a principle that goes all the way back to Abraham's encounter with God and the establishment of that wonderful covenant relationship.

Part of the covenant relationship promised blessing for obedience that would, in turn, produce blessing for others. Mr. Townsend echoed this principle when he stated, "We want lay people to be involved with Wycliffe because of the blessing it will be in their own lives as they are used to bless others through the translation of God's Word."

"And this ministry to lay people." said Al Ginty, President of Wycliffe Associates, "is precisely what WA is all about. I come to the office each day with the priority thought of how, or in what way, the lives of our now more than forty thousand WA members can be blessed so they can be a blessing. Our vision of where we feel the Lord is leading us as a service organization for lay people is expanding. We sense, for example, that the Lord is leading us to double our membership of involved WA'ers in the next five years. We have more hands-on service opportunities for construction, office, and personal skills in South and Central America, North America, the Pacific, Asia, Europe and Africa. But in the forefront of all this activity and program planning, in all the coordination of projects, in the nurturing of people, and in our prayers is the principle that the lay people who become involved with WA will be blessed and, in turn, be a blessing to Bible translation and to the Church at large."

Said Bruce Miller who leads WA's Missions Alive program, "We are changing people's lives, not just working with projects."

What a Difference a Team Makes documents the birth of an idea, an idea that has become an essential adjunct to Wycliffe's Bible translation ministry. It also tells the story of men, women and young people who seized an opportunity to serve God through their practical skills. And for many of them, the involvement has been, as one nuclear engineer said, "one of the most meaningful experiences of my life."

It's impossible, of course, to mention everyone who has played a role in WA's development over the past twenty years (1967-1987). Only in eternity will Wycliffe Associates' team effort be fully known. In the meantime, a special thank you to the thousands of Associates for blessing many through their prayers, generosity, God-given skills and commitment to the extension of God's kingdom through Bible translation.

Hugh Steven

Table of Contents

	Acknowledgments	
	Introduction	
One	Is There a Place for Lay People?	13
Two	Organizing the Home Front	25
Three	Adding Mission to Your Life	39
Four	The Faith Promise	53
Five	A Pause for New Direction	71
Six	Quality Programs with New Ideas	85
Seven	Golden Jubilee	95
Eight	Ministry Through Construction and Hospitality	115
Nine	What a Difference a Team Makes	135
Ten	Maturity Based on Prayer	149
	Postscript	167
	Introducing Martin Huyett	169
	Photos	171
	WA Lay Involvement Opportunities	187

Chapter One

Is There a Place for Lay People?

In 1967, popular American culture was erupting in violent protest. The general "revolt" pitted the young against the establishment. The nation was divided over Vietnam. President Lyndon Johnson could not visit any major city in the nation without being picketed by antiwar critics. The youth cried out not to trust anyone over thirty. And they echoed Pogo's famous dictum, "We have met the enemy and it is us." This general revolt against the establishment gave rise to the hippie generation who celebrated a "new freedom" of morality and questioned middle-class values. Their buzz-word was "depth-experience."

Thousands of young people tried to find their "depth experience" through a distorted use of drugs, sex and revolution. Many Christians responded to this spiritual turbulence by sponsoring hundreds of coffeehouses and parachurch activities. The phenomenal Jesus Movement also counterbalanced this widespread search for meaning and a true spiritual center.

It was in the midst of this great social upheaval that an opportunity for a different kind of "depth experience" was born. June 1967 marked the beginning of Wycliffe Associates. This fledgling organization would indeed provide a "depth experience" for thousands of lay people interested in Wycliffe's worldwide Bible translation ministry.

The early framers of the WA concept had four simple goals. One, to support and encourage Bible translators and other Wycliffe personnel in their task of providing God's Word for ethnic minorities. Two, to increase public awareness that lay people can be involved and become team members in Bible translation. Three, to provide and coordinate opportunities for volunteer technicians and other professional people to use their skills in practical, hands-on work projects. And four, to organize local WA chapters of men and women who would pray for and promote these objectives.

Wycliffe Associates' success in achieving these goals is now a matter of public record. God has expanded and allowed WA to minister in ways undreamed of at its inception. Under the visionary leadership of John Bender, Vice President for the Construction Ministry, there are construction crews, telephone installers and utility men who dig for clean water in such distant places as Irian Jaya, Senegal, Guatemala, Peru and the Philippines. Even as you read this, WA construction crews are at work building clinics, hangars for JAARS airplanes, missionary and language-helper housing, and centers at home and abroad for linguistic and Bible translation workshops. What was once said of Great Britain, that the sun never set on its empire, is literally true of WA.

The hub of this creative worldwide ministry is an eleven-thousand-square-foot, unpretentious but efficient office building located on a former orange grove in Orange, California. WA's president, Al Ginty, the man most responsible the past ten years for innovative growth and development, has a staff of almost sixty people. Some, like Sarah Pease, have been with WA since its first executive secretary, Bill Butler, and his wife Bettie worked out of a walk-up, second-story office building in Santa Ana, California. Others include longtime staffer John Bender (Vice President for Construction Ministries), Wes Syverson (Utilities Director), Mary Cates (former Director of Publications Ministries and presently Prayer Ministries Director), Dave Crawford (Vice President for Finance and Personnel), Southeast Area Director Peter Brouillette, and South Central Area Director Richard Grahn. Relatively new WA staff additions include Mike Yoder, former Banquet Ministries Coordinator and presently the new Director of Publications Ministries, and Bruce Miller, Director of Missions Alive.

Besides Ric Winter, Senior Construction Superintendent, and Lonnie Waldner, Foreign Projects Coordinator, there are thirteen construction superintendents and assistants, plus U.S. and special projects coordinators, utilities superintendents and more.

Like the prayer ministry that undergirds all personnel, long-time staffers Roger and Barbara Petrey, a devoted husband and wife team, direct the mailroom ministry. Other husband and wife teams include John Bender and Liz, Wes Syverson and Mary Ann, Al Ginty and Vivian. These wives are deeply committed and play a strategic role in WA's office ministry.

Thus, on WA's twentieth birthday, it seemed fitting to remember the beginning and all the ways God has led since then. WA's history pays tribute to God Who is ever active in the affairs of his people. All kinds of people—doctors, plumbers, farmers, lawyers, school teachers, students, housewives, secretaries, business executives, builders and nuclear engineers—all working side-by-side, united by the single theme: "That all peoples should have the Word of God made available to them in whatever language it may be best known to them" (John Wycliffe, 1320-1384).

Twenty years ago, however, the notion of Wycliffe Bible Translators (WBT) having an official lay organization was received by WBT's home office with some skepticism. Mr. Townsend, of course, understood the important contribution lay people could make to the Bible translation ministry and always looked for creative ways to involve them.

Wycliffe's early history, therefore, is replete with the names of laymen who played a strategic role in its development and direction. Men like William G. Nyman, Wycliffe's first treasurer, and his daughters, Mary Ann and Eleanor (Tutty). And Amos Baker, an oil man from Oklahoma; Tom Hayward, a hardware merchant from Siloam Springs, Arkansas; Tom Trowbridge, Tom Crowell, Bill Wyatt, Bob Rensch, Armon Dawson, Henderson Belk—the list goes on and on until one could fill an entire book with the names of laymen who played strategic roles in shaping Wycliffe's history. In most cases these men and women were involved informally, and almost all were recruited directly or indirectly by Mr. Townsend.

It wasn't until 1966, however, when Dr. Dale W. Kietzman joined Wycliffe's home office (then in Santa Ana, California) as Extension Director, that the seeds sown by Mr. Townsend and others began to blossom into what is known today as Wycliffe Associates. But to understand more clearly how these seeds were planted, we must step back to 1952.

In late 1951 and early 1952, Dr. Dick Pittman, then director of Wycliffe's work in the Philippines, with his wife Kay and their children, furloughed in Wheaton, Illinois, a suburb of Chicago. Building on Mr. Townsend's long habit of inviting laymen to become involved in Wycliffe, Dick shared the Wycliffe story with as many as he could.

"Soon," said Dick, "there was a special group of men and women who showed the seriousness of their resolve to be practically involved with Bible translation by forming themselves into a group called the Chicago-Wheaton Committee."

In the group were two Wheaton College professors, Drs. Clarence Hale and Bob Stone. These men gave many years to Wycliffe's cause, making it possible for Wycliffe personnel to speak in Wheaton's chapel and conduct special seminars and classes on campus. Another committee member was Bea Stybr who gathered a selection of towels and linens for Wycliffe workers from the Chicago area. This practical ministry later gave birth to WA's celebrated Linen Closet. As of this writing, hundreds of Wycliffe workers and their families have received complete sets of quality towels and bed linens, either on their return from, or prior to, their assignments.

Also in Chicago at that time, and a member of this special group, was Bill Wyatt, Circulation Manager for the *Chicago American* (a Hearst publication). Bill, born of British parents, had lived in Belize (British Honduras) and remembered the spiritual poverty of the many ethnic peoples, particularly those without Scriptures in their language. He, therefore, welcomed the opportunity to serve temporarily in 1952 as Wycliffe's official representative in Chicago.

One of the first challenges Bill Wyatt faced in 1952 was how to effectively distribute a new Wycliffe movie that had been filmed in Mexico and Peru by Dr. Irwin Moon of the Moody Institute of Science. No one foresaw the enormous impact this film would have in influencing a whole generation of people to commit themselves to Bible translation. The film, *O for a Thousand Tongues,* has since become a Wycliffe classic.

Ill health had brought William G. Nyman to California from Chicago where he operated a successful lumber business. In 1942, when Wycliffe Bible Translators was officially incorporated, the second-story apartment over Mr. Nyman's garage in Glendale, California, became WBT's home office. William Nyman had offered to do whatever he could to help and that "whatever" turned out to be twenty years of wise financial counsel as the first secretary-treasurer of Wycliffe Bible Translators and the Summer Institute of Linguistics. Clearly he was God's instrument to hold Wycliffe's fiscal reins. Yet, in the minds of some, he was almost too conservative. He saw little value in spending money on advertising or movie production. His energies were given to saving money.

Bill Wyatt, on the other hand, wanted to push ahead to alert the public to the need and opportunities for service. Working without a computer or central mailing list, Bill simply drove into a town and made personal phone calls to local pastors. Said Dale Kietzman when he returned from Peru to be the official Wycliffe presence in Chicago, "When I came into the little office Bill had rented on the second story of the condemned 153 building at Moody Bible Institute, I found a stack of Yellow Pages from telephone directories—all of them church listings. This was Bill's mailing list. To be sure it was unorthodox, but it worked."

What also worked was the Chicago-Wheaton Committee. When Bill Wyatt took a leave of absence from his job at the *Chicago American* to more fully involve himself with the distribution of the film, the Committee picked up Bill's salary as well as the office rent.

As the months passed, Bill began getting more and more bookings based on the film's popularity. The California home office then asked him to arrange deputation speaking tours for Wycliffe workers on furlough. Bill, assisted by Milton Gabler, a Wycliffe worker on sick leave, thus began arranging planned itineraries for Wycliffe speakers.

When Dale Kietzman relieved Bill Wyatt as WBT's Chicago Extension Director in 1953, he continued using the resources of the Chicago-Wheaton Committee and enlisted others like Dick Bowman and Bob Rensch (late father of Dr. Calvin Rensch, who was then working among the Chinantec people of southern Mexico). Said Dale, "These men, eager to serve, were the nucleus of what was later to become Wycliffe Associates." However, the problem of how to involve the more than two hundred laymen who wanted a mission-field experience remained unsolved.

Mr. Townsend involved people by inviting them to tour the SIL headquarters in Mexico City and visit one or two ethnic villages. Often this included the Aztec village of Tetelcingo where he had worked. In the mid-fifties, Dale built on this idea and the Chicago office advertised tours to Mexico for pastors.

These Pastors Tours provided a splendid opportunity for church leaders to broaden their experience of cross-cultural missions in general and Bible translation in particular. Wycliffe gained many friends from these special tours, but they were limited to pastors, or so-called professional Christians. Even if laymen did take a trip and returned home full of enthusiasm, there was no mechanism to involve them in an ongoing ministry. (Later, under WA's leadership, the emphasis changed and the Pastors Tours became Guest Tours and included both men and women.)

During the decade of the mid-fifties to mid-sixties, other lay representatives and committees sprang up across the United States. Dr. Phil and Barbara Grossman, with their colleagues Wilson and Vivian Stiteler, served on the Philadelphia Committee. Phil, like Bill Wyatt, became Wycliffe's official lay representative. Armon Dawson, an Indiana real estate developer, gave himself unselfishly to make Wycliffe known wherever and whenever he could. He also played an important role in alleviating serious land problems for a group of Otomi Indians in central Mexico and helped secure land for the important SIL translation center in Ixmiquilpan, Mexico.

Lawrence Routh had involved himself with the Jungle Aviation and Radio Service (JAARS) program at Waxhaw, North Carolina. When the need arose to retire the debt on the Wycliffe Pavilion at the New York World's Fair in 1964-65, he organized a series of fundraising banquets and called them "Operation 2000." The name was a reference to what was then commonly believed to be the remaining number of ethnic groups needing Scripture translation. (That number now stands at three thousand five hundred fifteen.) Once again a layman under the leading of the Holy Spirit helped solve a critical problem.

During the next decade, 1956-1966, Wycliffe experienced a remarkable surge in personnel. In 1956, Wycliffe's membership stood at five hundred ninety-three. By 1966 it had grown to one thousand seven hundred eighty-five. This amazing surge of spiritual interest swept across America. Wrote one observer, "The United States was being stirred by a religious consciousness the like of which it has not seen since the turn of the century." Much of that stirring came from young people who, after a long, empty search for meaning and fulfillment (often in the wrong places), finally found truth in a personal love relationship with Jesus Christ and wanted to share that love in meaningful service. Bible translation offered these young people a remarkable challenge plus the opportunity to involve themselves in a ministry greater than themselves, a ministry that would call forth the best they had to offer.

In 1966, therefore, Wycliffe's energies were devoted mainly to absorbing, training and allocating its rapidly expanding personnel. Public relations, extension offices and the necessary financial support for workers (who are responsible for their own prayer and financial support) had not kept pace. If Wycliffe was to meet its stated goals of reaching the world's ethnic minority groups with the Gospel through Bible translation, the decade of the seventies and on into the eighties would require an even greater increase in personnel. Clearly Wycliffe faced a public relations crisis of mammoth proportions. To meet these critical demands, the Wycliffe board turned once again to Dale Kietzman. This time he was asked to head up the Extension and Deputation Department for the entire United States.

When Dale returned to Wycliffe's home office, then in Santa Ana, he reopened several regional offices and coordinated them with others functioning independently. With its rapid ten-year growth, Wycliffe had grown more complex and he wanted qualified people to head up each regional office, people with field experience and familiar with Wycliffe's policies and practices.

There was no question in Dale's mind that an innovative way to fulfill the mandate of the Great Commission was to involve a corps of self-supporting lay people, who, in reality, would be lay missionaries. But Dale, besides being a visionary, was also a pragmatist. He knew that with his limited budget of twenty-five thousand dollars (a modest film production would cost double that amount), he couldn't possibly develop the needed public relations program.

Said Dale, "Over the years I had met people who were willing to pray and give, and this is necessary. We can't operate without prayer, and we certainly can't operate without money. But from my experience in Chicago, I knew there were lay people who would work hard, travel, make phone calls and print materials without ever sending a bill, and I needed that kind of commitment and support. These people burned deeply in my heart. They wanted something more—a hands-on mission experience—and I identified with their frustration at not being part of the action."

Dale, a keen observer of human nature and an anthropologist by training, knew that to deny people a significant part in implementing a cause contributes little to their development. He, like Mr. Townsend, and certainly the current WA administration, wanted the lay person both to serve and be enriched through that service.

He openly shared his vision of more lay involvement with WBT's home office staff and administration and asked them to make this a matter of prayer. Many did, although, at the time, few envisioned how such a lay organization would work.

In response to the problem, Danny O'Brien, then editor of Wycliffe's *Translation* † magazine, mentioned a man who had come through the office several months earlier. "He was impressed with Wycliffe," said Danny, "and visited every office to see if there was some way he could be a part of what Wycliffe was doing. None of the

---

† This has now been changed to *In Other Words*.

offices, however, knew how to incorporate him."

"What's his name?" asked Dale.

"He's a relative of our Al Graham," said Danny. "His name is Bill Butler."

Chapter Two

Organizing the Home Front

I t happened in Scripture, and it frequently happens to many of us. We experience periods when we fail to perceive God's intervention in our lives. Then, suddenly, an event, a chance meeting, a single word or sentence changes forever how we think, act, or conduct our lives.

It happened to Bill Butler. Handsome, with vigorous health, he had a good job, a beautiful wife, two teenage sons and a home in the sun in San Diego, California. But then one day, right before his eyes, his best friend was killed in a boating accident. This shock, plus the reality that one day he himself would also die, opened the way for his friend and business partner, Paul Sutherland, to lead him to the Lord. For the next four years, Bill and his wife Bettie immersed themselves in the outreach and ministry of Scott Memorial Church. Bill was also involved in Paul Sutherland's political campaign as a candidate for the California state legislature.

One afternoon while Bill was delivering political handbills for Paul, he noticed a parked truck with the name "Wycliffe Bible Translators" painted on its side. Standing beside the truck was a man Bill recognized as a recent speaker at Scott Memorial. It was Jack Kendall, a telephone engineer who enthusiastically spoke in many churches about the need for men to become involved in the practical ministry of installing water, electrical and telephone (WET) systems at Wycliffe's SIL centers around the world. (Later Jack would become WA's first WET director.)

Both men exchanged pleasantries and Bill learned more about Wycliffe's worldwide ministry. Several days later, Joe and Mickey Girard, an affable Wycliffe couple en route to Waxhaw, North Carolina, stopped by Bill's office to say good-bye. In the course of conversation, Joe challenged Bill to consider Wycliffe as an option for service. Bill explained that he was involved with Campus Crusade and Paul Sutherland's political campaign. "But I'm open to whatever the Lord has for me," he said.

Despite his best efforts, Bill's candidate lost the election. Now with extra time on his hands, he remembered Joe Girard's challenge and drove ninety miles north from San Diego to Santa Ana to see if Wycliffe had a place for him to serve. It turned out to be woefully less encouraging than he had expected. Bill met with three of the top administrators and they graciously listened to his reasons for wanting to become a part of what Wycliffe was doing, but since Bill didn't want to enter Wycliffe through the normal membership channels of SIL and Jungle Camp, the administrators didn't know how to make use of his skills. Discouraged and bewildered, Bill was led to the door of the Santa Ana office by the then-Assistant Extension Director, Dr. Rudy Renfer. "If you are truly interested in us," said Rudy, "find out more about us and what we are about."

"How would I do that?" asked Bill.

"One way would be to take one of our tours to Mexico," said Rudy.

Bill took Rudy's suggestion and he and Bettie left for Mexico in February 1966. It was a memorable experience. They were particularly impressed with Ken and Elaine Jacobs's ministry among the Chamula† people in the state of Chiapas. In some ways, however, the experience frustrated him. Now he was more convinced than ever he should somehow use his energies to further the cause of Bible translation. But when he again approached Wycliffe administrators in Santa Ana, no one seemed to know exactly how to plug him into any existing program.

Thus, when Dale Kietzman phoned Bill in the early weeks of 1967, his enthusiasm for Wycliffe had cooled considerably. Nevertheless, Bill, with his friend Paul Sutherland, met with Dale and Danny O'Brien at WBT's Santa Ana office.

Dale spoke briefly about his past involvement with laymen in Chicago and of their unique contribution to Wycliffe's ministry. He asked Bill if he would help him start a lay organization.

"You can't be serious," said Bill. "I came to Wycliffe a year ago and offered my services to do this very thing, but no one seemed interested."

"Things have changed since then," said Dale. "I believe we have a place for you. I accepted this appointment with a burden to start an organization that would utilize laymen and their skills in a way we haven't in the past. We need a coordinated group of men and women from all across the United States— and perhaps even into Canada and elsewhere—who will pray in a concerned way for Wycliffe's work. We need people who will be willing to show a Wycliffe film

---

† See *They Dared to be Different* by Hugh Steven, the story of the birth of the Chamula church. Available through the Bookroom of Wycliffe Bible Translators, Huntington Beach, CA, 92647.

and provide hospitality for our workers as they travel on furlough.

"In a word, we need an organization that will stand behind our workers on the field and give them logistical support in areas where the layman is most skilled. Often our translators are required to build a house, or they may want to be involved in community development but aren't trained. Or if they are able to do these things, such activity often takes them away from their primary work of Bible translation. My burden has been to somehow identify laymen and their skills and match them with needs on the field. There are a lot more possibilities, but at this point, I'm not exactly sure how we'll implement them. However, I'd like to begin and would like you to explore the possibilities with me. One of the first things we have to do is lay out our plans and convince the Wycliffe administration that the idea will work."

In an effort to lay the groundwork, gain a consensus and convince Wycliffe's administration that a lay organization would work within the framework of Wycliffe's policies, Dale and Bill met once a week for a planning lunch with top Wycliffe administrators.

After about ten weeks, Bill once again broke through what he considered excessive bureaucratic fog and indecision. Before the meeting, Bill approached Dale and said, "Look, I'm tired of coming to these meetings. We don't seem to be getting anywhere."

"I agree with you," said Dale. "Let's see if we can't turn this around today."

After the luncheon, Dale said, "During these weeks of discussion, we've all agreed with the concept of a lay organization. We have considered the legal implications and Robert Bartholomew, a layman already working in the office, has thoroughly researched other auxiliary organizations to examine their relationships to parent organizations. I believe we must now test our ideas. These meetings, then, are no longer necessary, but we will report our progress to you on a regular basis."

And that's the way it happened. No official Wycliffe board action. Just some administrators who said, "Okay, we'll let you test the idea"—and, of course, Bill Butler's audacious faith.

The following Monday morning, Dale arrived first at the Wycliffe headquarters housed in an old two-story church building in Santa Ana.† To his surprise, he found Bill sitting on the doorstep.

"What are you doing here so early on a Monday morning?" asked Dale.

"I quit my job on Friday and I'm here to work," said Bill. "I want to begin that test we decided on last week and I'm trusting the Lord to make it work."

Astonished that Bill had acted with such forthright determination and faith, Dale invited Bill inside. "I don't know where we'll put you, but we'll find a spot somewhere."

In those days, every nook and cranny of the old church building seemed occupied with a desk or work table. Desks for secretaries, and whoever else needed workspace, were set up in the long main hallway. It was here, on a battered desk in the main hallway, that Bill Butler, WA's first Executive Secretary, began to plan WA's direction and strategy.

Those early days were filled with both apprehension and wonder. Apprehension came from those who opposed establishing a completely new organization of laymen who would speak on Wycliffe's behalf. They viewed this as a dangerous departure from the established

---

† WBT's headquarters moved to Huntington Beach in March 1974.

pattern of member orientation. After all, they reasoned, only a person with Wycliffe's prescribed training and orientation could speak authoritatively about the challenges and opportunities of a cross-cultural ministry. Dale only partially agreed with this reasoning. He knew the complexity of Wycliffe's policies and assured skeptics that only qualified representatives would serve as spokesmen.

The wonder, on the other hand, came from how God was bringing events and people together to meet the needs of this new lay organization. One of the first needs was office space. This was supplied by the Wycliffe office manager, Granville Dougherty, when he secured the second floor of an old office building a block from headquarters. Bill immediately moved from the hallway into his new office. During the first four months of occupancy, Bill set up an army cot in the back room of his office, cooked and slept there during the week, returning home to San Diego on weekends.

By spring 1967, Bill, Bettie and their two sons had moved from San Diego into a low-rent apartment in nearby Orange. WA's first full-time secretary, Sarah Pease, handled the routine office load which was beginning to mushroom.

By now the name Wycliffe Associates was agreed upon as the organization's official name. The name, "Lollards," had been considered in honor of the itinerant or wandering preachers established by John Wycliffe to carry out his vision of making the Scriptures accessible to every man in his own tongue. No one is certain when the name "Wycliffe Associates" was adopted. What stands out in the memory of those involved is that the name "Wycliffe Associates" emerged by common consent.

Almost on the heels of the move to their "new"

offices, Bill and Dale met Arthur DeMoss, a chief executive of Valley Forge Insurance Company. Like Bill, he had been on a Pastors Tour to Mexico and had been deeply impressed by what he had experienced. When Dale and Bill shared their vision for an organization that would encourage laymen to use their business skills for the cause of Bible translation, Arthur DeMoss said he would help and asked specifically how they were going to raise the necessary capital.

"Wycliffe has given us a one-time use of their mailing list," said Dale. "It's our plan to involve as many people nationwide by offering a charter membership into Wycliffe Associates for ten dollars per year. For that fee, new Wycliffe Associates members will receive a handsome, specially-designed lapel pin and a newsletter that will inform them of involvement opportunities. We are planning to organize WA chapters nationwide. There are some other things we want to do but they haven't been worked out as yet."

As the men talked and Arthur DeMoss learned that Bill and his wife Bettie had given up their home and left their business, which meant they had abandoned their ability to earn a large salary, he expressed amazement at their vision and faith. "I have on my staff a young man who is tops in direct-mail solicitation. His name is Gaylor Briley and I would like to offer his services to you. And as part of my involvement, I will pick up the tab for his salary."

This clear provision from God posed only one problem. The fledgling organization had no capital to pay for the layout, design and printing of a first mailing to approximately thirty thousand people.

Writers of history usually hold up the actions and choices of individuals as indicators of their true temperament and character. Sometimes, however, we become puzzled by certain discrepancies, either by deeds that don't match a person's words, or, like Bill Butler, deeds that far outstrip a person's words.

Bill had run a car-leasing dealership and his actions and body language epitomized those of a car salesman. He was persistent, persuasive, impatient with too much reflection and often frustrated over indecision. But these were the very leadership qualities needed to take an organization beginning at ground zero and make it fly. Almost without hesitation, he offered to take out a personal ninety-day bank loan of thirteen thousand dollars to cover the printing and mailing expenses and to help pay for a trip he, Dale and Dr. Rudy Renfer (who was now acting as WA's first president), were taking around the United States to introduce WA to the Christian community.

This was indeed a bold step of faith. It was a step that many said would never work. From the beginning, however, it was obvious that Bill was not bound by the status quo. If he had followed Wycliffe's conservative fiscal policy of paying as you go, such a loan, in all probability, would never have been approved. But this was Wycliffe Associates and its management would be different from the parent organization.

WBT's policy then (and today, with some slight modification) was to supply information about a member's personal financial support or project needs only when specifically requested. Such a policy, of course, made little sense to the pragmatic businessman who argued, "How can I help you if you don't tell me what your needs are?"

Wycliffe Associates meant to modify the policy by first asking the Wycliffe organization what their specific needs were, and then tactfully make them known to its constituency. How this would be accomplished had not yet been fully formulated except for one vehicle—the *WA Newsletter.* This media piece would be oversized and printed on bright goldenrod, "so that no one can miss it," said Dale.

The response to WA's first mailing for charter members exceeded anyone's expectation. When Bill's bank note became due, the WA charter membership stood at thirteen hundred. The treasury had a balance of thirteen thousand two hundred dollars—just enough for Bill to meet his debt obligation. Later in a written report, Bill said, "The response to our 'invitation-to-join' mail has been very strong. The ages of membership run from thirteen to eighty-nine years. The honor of being the youngest member goes to Bob Hart of Costa Mesa, California. The very first to join were Mr. and Mrs. Harold Larson of Portland, Oregon. In January of this year [1967], Mr. Larson heard about the plans for forming Wycliffe Associates and sent his check even before we had any printed material to send him."

By the end of their first year, WA had grown to four thousand four hundred. Local WA chapters number- ed forty-six, organized or partially organized. The WA Guest Tours program had sent twenty-four people on a cross-cultural experience to Mexico and other countries. Forty Associates had responded to WA's first construction ministry projects in Alaska and at the JAARS headquarters in Waxhaw, North Carolina. Five Associates were working on long-term assignments as guest workers on the field. Joseph Profita, WA's first secretary-treasurer, gave a simple balance sheet report listing projects and disburse- ments and a black balance of eighteen thousand twenty dollars in the bank. Additionally, Bill and Dale made their first baby steps toward implementing what would eventually become one of WA's fundamental ministries—the Faith Promise Banquet.

The first flush of letters from Associate members resounded with high hopes and enthusiasm. "I am honored to be asked to join. After three weeks in Central and South America as part of your guest tour, my understanding of Third World missions has forever been changed. I am so excited about the WA program I could shout!" One Oklahoman who had spent time in Peru said, "Thank you, WA, for providing me a vehicle through which I can tangibly use my skills as a way to minister to tribal peoples."

Remarkably, the WA concept struck a responsive chord in the hearts of hundreds of people. It was all the more remarkable because this was the mid-sixties when many so-called Christians said contemporary Christianity has lost its imperative for missions. It was in an age when it was popularly conceived that there were few absolutes. Yet all indicators pointed toward the success of an organization that would give lay people a unique oportunity to use their natural gifts and abilities in a positive ministry.

There was, however, a problem. To make this idea work, WA needed a vehicle to reach a wider Christian constituency. WBT had given them a one-time use of their mailing list. Now they had to develop their own. A few weeks after that first mailing, fewer and fewer new charter memberships arrived. The mailing had peaked.

One day in an informal brainstorming session about the problem, Bill offhandedly said to Dale, "Let's have some dinner meetings."

"What would you do at these dinner meetings?" asked Dale.

Candidly Bill said he didn't know exactly what should happen or how the meetings might be executed.

Dale assured Bill that his idea was sound, but said

they must have a plan. "You know," continued Dale, "for several years now I have received a letter once a year from Dr. Oswald J. Smith, pastor of The Peoples Church, Toronto, Canada, asking me why Wycliffe doesn't adopt a faith-promise plan for giving. And every year I write back and tell him that I don't see how we could do this because we don't have a mechanism for keeping track of our donors. I always ask him how we can do this, but I never hear back from him. Now, however, I think WA could handle such a program."

Dale then suggested to Bill that he schedule a series of spring dinner meetings for 1968. "In the meantime, I'll contact Dr. Smith and tell him that his opportunity has arrived. I'll ask him to come and show us how to put on a series of faith promise banquets."

Dr. Smith accepted Dale Kietzman's invitation and for several years, in the company of Johnny Mitchell, a former business colleague of Bill's who joined WA as the Southwestern Field Representative, did indeed show WA how to do it. One method was through a film produced by the Moody Institute of Science film department entitled, *How God Taught Me to Give.*

This has since become a film of great historic value and was used powerfully during the early days of the WA banquets to challenge thousands of people to trust God for a surprise gift of money over and above their normal giving that could be used for a specific WA project.

In June 1968, the bright goldenrod *WA Newsletter* gave a brief, almost stilted report on the outcome of those first banquets.

A series of banquets were held in Oregon to help purchase a float plane for Wycliffe's use on the rivers of Northern Brazil. Our goal was to

raise fifty thousand dollars. Dr. Oswald J. Smith,
revered missionary statesman, was the speaker
for these meetings. One thousand five hundred
sixty-one people attended the banquets. The
Lord blessed and we went over the top.

One little-known fact is that as a result of Dr. Smith's
involvement, WA and Wycliffe doubled the number of
donors in the state of Oregon in one two-week period.
    Under the theme, "Wycliffe Associates, Field Involve-
ment for the Layman," Don and Nadine Burns, energetic Wycliffe literacy workers among the Quechua
people in the Peruvian Andes, toured with two Quechua
believers, Fernando and Lucio, who gave their personal
testimonies of how they came to faith in Christ.
Afterward, Don shared the need for building a center to
train Quechua leaders in evangelism and community
development. This simple beginning and format became a model which would be refined and developed
over the next twenty years to profoundly bless both the
giver and receiver.
    Another couple who played a significant role in
developing the faith-promise banquet series was Al
and Eunice Williams, then working in Mexico as hosts
and public relations officers to the many visitors and
dignitaries who visited the SIL center in Tlalpan
outside Mexico City. Recounting the successful banquet
series held in Oregon, Bill Butler invited Al and Eunice
to conduct eight banquets in their native New England
states.
    "It will never work in conservative New England,"
said Al.
    Flashing his characteristic, never-take-no-for-an
answer smile, Bill said, "You people in Wycliffe
don't realize how much people love Wycliffe and

Bible translation!"

Accepting this challenge, Al and Eunice invited Manuel Arenas, a Totonac Indian from Mexico and co-translator of the Totonac New Testament,† to be their speaker and began their banquet series in Rhode Island. The rest is history. Years later, Al and Eunice joined WA as full-time directors in the North Central area. Manuel has since become a frequent banquet speaker and unofficial spokesman for both WA and Wycliffe.

Perhaps the one verse of Scripture that characterized WA's central attitude in those first days (and even now), is the discourse in Luke 22:27 where Jesus says, "I am among you as one who serves." From a casual reading of WA's first year-end report, one could almost catch the electric excitement of those serving. One couple from Denver, Colorado, donated a forty-horsepower outboard motor to be used in Peru. An 81-year-old artist from Texas paid her own way to Papua New Guinea and used her talents illustrating primers and other reading materials.

Many Associates served in quiet, unassuming ways. One woman opened her home to a returning Wycliffe family. Still another donated her time by proofreading Wycliffe materials for publication. Others gave books for field libraries. Musical instruments were donated for Wycliffe children on the field. That first year, seven automobiles were donated for furloughing Wycliffe workers. The list goes on—WA responding to a storm-damaged building in Central America, a medical fund established for an Otomi Indian girl born without

---

† See *Manuel* and *Manuel, the Continuing Story* by Hugh Steven. Available through the WBT Book Room, Huntington Beach, CA, 92647.

ears—people serving, giving and experiencing the truth
of Jesus' words, "it is much better to give than to
receive."

In tribute to their extraordinary first-year contribution
to Bible translation, Wycliffe's founder William
Cameron Townsend wrote WA a letter of appreciation.
Part of it read:

> Wycliffe has long needed an organized
> channel for greater home front participation
> and active personal support on the field. During
> this past year, Wycliffe Associates has come
> onto the scene to supply a great need. The
> accomplishments under God during this begin-
> ning year have been most encouraging.
>
> I personally join Dr. Renfer and the members
> of the Wycliffe Associates Board in thanks-
> giving to God, in thanks to all Wycliffe Associates,
> and for a special word of appreciation to Execu-
> tive Secretary Bill Butler, for the untiring efforts
> which have given impetus to this beginning
> year.
>
> W. Cameron Townsend
> General Director
> Wycliffe Bible Translators, Inc.

Chapter Three

Adding Mission to Your Life

In June 1987, the WA board of trustees selected the theme, "Adding Mission to Your Life," for their annual meeting. To commemorate that event as well as WA's twentieth year, Mary Cates and her editorial staff prepared a special anniversary bulletin highlighting the amazing contours of WA's twenty-year ministry. One section began by quoting Dr. Rudy Renfer, WA's first president:

> From its beginning, lay people have been the mainstay of Wycliffe Bible Translators. June 1, 1967, marked the beginning of Wycliffe Associates, the formal auxiliary organization of lay people dedicated to broadening the home front and field support of Wycliffe Bible Translators.
>
> To draw a poignant phrase from the annals of modern missionary history, Wycliffe Associates has been designed to more effectively 'hold the ropes' for the Wycliffe Bible translators.
>
> In 1792, William Carey said, 'I will go to India if you will hold the ropes at home.' He had preached on winning the lost. . . .His preaching and prayer led to personal involvement. The era

of modern missions was born. Who can measure
the dimension of that beginning?

The nature of an anniversary is to celebrate. Usually
the celebration centers around a certain achievement
or growth. And that's what this volume is about—the
celebration of WA's expanded ministry and of those
who have "held the ropes" and thereby made an eternal
difference in the lives of Wycliffe workers and the
people they serve. It also chronicles the special joy
many Associates experienced as they discovered that
by serving others they are serving their Lord.

It has been said that those willing to do what God
expects often experience things no one thought possible.
This is the testimony of scores of Associates who, when
asked what their personal involvement with WA has
meant, said: "I always wanted to serve the Lord as a
missionary and WA gave me the opportunity. I never
dreamed the fellowship could be so rich. We have made
wonderful new friends. Being involved in a concrete
way [with WA] has given us more meaning in our lives
and made us richer."

Two of those who were enriched and forever changed
through their WA involvement are Rey and Margie
Johnson of Fullerton, California. After their return
from a guest tour of Mexico, they, like the Butlers,
caught the heartbeat of Bible translation. Like Bill, Rey
felt he possessed certain business skills that could be
used effectively to advance this cause.

Rey's first visit to Wycliffe headquarters in Santa
Ana almost duplicated Bill's a few months before. Rey
presented himself to several administrators, and each
said they didn't have a place for him. Dr. Benjamin
Elson, Wycliffe's then Executive Vice President, did,
however, suggest that Rey contact Wycliffe Associates.

"It's a new organization that's just getting under way. Perhaps they'll have something more suited to what you want."

About a week later, Rey attended a WA board meeting with his friend Jim Beam, a newly-appointed WA board member. Before the meeting ended, Rey was elected as WA's treasurer. This action proved both wise and fortuitous. Rey, and later with his wife Margie, gave over ten years of wise counsel, service and direction, particularly during the early developmental period in WA's history.

A review of WA's beginning months reveals an amazing amount of energy being generated in the implementation of new ideas at several different levels. "And," said Paul Robbins, an insurance broker and member of the WA board, "Bill Butler could pump out more new ideas about how to serve God through WA than would be possible to expedite in a lifetime!"

Ideas, the lifeblood of any organization, had to come from key people who could transform them into reality. Those key people who served on the first Board of Trustees, and whom history has recorded as WA's Founding Fathers, were ten. They included Dale Kietzman, who functioned as WA's secretary and held several prominent WBT posts. This was a critical position since it was his responsibility to interpret Wycliffe policy and principles to WA and to act as communicator and liaison between the two organizations. There was President Bill Butler. Lorin Griset, then mayor of Santa Ana, California, and nephew of William Cameron Townsend, served as vice chairman. Lorin possessed great insight into Wycliffe since his earliest memories of his famous Uncle Cam were the marvelous stories he told on his return from Mexico of God's working in and through Wycliffe and SIL. Lorin also served on WBT's international board and was active in the community at large.

Joe Profita, a management counselor from Tustin, California, added his quiet but sparkling wit to the board. Rey Johnson, as already stated, was treasurer and soon became known for his dynamic leadership (he would serve as WA's president during 1975 and 1976). He also was known for his selfless generosity both to individual Wycliffe members and to the WA organization. Dr. Rudy Renfer stepped down from the WA presidency to assume his duties as WBT's Development Secretary, but gave firm and insightful leadership during those first few months of WA's inception. Jim Beam, a banker from Orange, gave valuable financial direction, as did Everett Sweem, a land developer from Sacramento and, from San Diego, Bill's spiritual mentor and confidant, Paul Sutherland.

Though not considered as WA's "official" founding fathers, two other board members, elected in 1970, gave creative leadership and wise counsel to an organization that had learned how to fly almost before it could walk. From W. Lafayette, Indiana, came Paul Von Tobel, president of a building-supply chain. Paul had gained an understanding of Wycliffe's ministry by firsthand observation on several trips to South America and Alaska. (He oversaw and directed the twenty-one tons of building materials needed to construct the first SIL Alaska Center.) Like Paul, Nathan Bruckhart, a land developer and realtor from Akron, Pennsylvania, brought to the WA board a broad base of business experience.

While the board members met to discuss and formulate policies, day-to-day operations were managed by Bill and his staff of five. These included Business Manager Doug Meland, a former Wycliffe translator in

Brazil; Jerry Long, editor of *WA Newsletter*, a Wycliffe member with field experience in Peru; Bill's wife Bettie, who served as his personal secretary, assisted by Donna Sharp; and WA's first and longest employee, Sarah Pease, who still works with WA in Orange.

A foundational principle for all WA projects, programs and banquet series was that they be undergirded by prayer. Associates could be invited to pray for anything from a new cook stove in a Center kitchen, to a translation team entering their first allocation, or the health of a specific Wycliffe worker.

Often prayer requests listed in the monthly *WA Newsletter* acted as centerpieces for WA chapter meetings. Without an organized WA chapter, some people, like Mrs. Elsie Holmes of South Porcupine, Ontario, Canada, began her own unique WA outreach. Elsie's special prayer interest for Wycliffe workers was highlighted in the October 1969 *WA Newsletter:*

> To celebrate Canada's centennial year, Mrs. Elsie Holmes wrote to one hundred Canadian missionaries serving with Wycliffe. When she began receiving answers to her letters, she said, "I was so thrilled with the response to my first hundred letters, I just had to keep writing."
>
> Elsie Holmes first became interested in Wycliffe Bible Translators after reading *Through Gates of Splendor.*
>
> "The book so challenged me," said Elsie, "I felt I had to do something positive for the Lord."
>
> Elsie began by writing directly to Rachel Saint working among the Aucas in Ecuador. "I wanted current information and prayer requests," she said, "and I wanted to get to know Rachel Saint better."

Both of these desires have come true. Rachel was happy for a concerned prayer partner, Mrs. Holmes wrote after receiving her first letter, and since then has kept her informed about important developments among the Aucas. Because of their vigorous correspondence, both have developed a warm friendship.

Letters festooned with exotic stamps from Vietnam, the Philippines, Ecuador, Central America and other countries, soon found their way into the modest home in South Porcupine. With each one came news and prayer items. These Mrs. Holmes shared regularly with her friends at the Wednesday night, church prayer meeting.

"As we prayed for Hank Blood in Vietnam," said Mrs. Holmes, "the Goheens in Central America, Rachel in Ecuador and others, things happened in our meeting. People who previously had shown no interest in missions suddenly became deeply concerned. The letters helped us to become more personally involved with Wycliffe missionaries, and it was as if we knew many of them personally. The Lord further rewarded us by making the prayer meetings one of the most refreshing hours in the week."

As incredible as it may seem, and as much as some would shrink from the responsibility, God's love is mediated through human relationships. And this has been central in WA's twenty-year ministry. This is seen in their ordinary day-to-day encounters, and in the extraordinary projects that present themselves to the WA administrators.

One such extraordinary mission project dubbed as

WA's first "emergency mission of mercy" revolved around an incident that occurred one dark night in late 1967 among the Chamula people in the highlands of Southern Mexico. About forty men descended upon a solitary hut set in the middle of a cornfield. Silently the men squirted gasoline onto the thick thatch roof and then set it ablaze with the flick of a match.

Inside the hut five people slept—five-year-old Abelina, her three sisters and eighteen-year-old Paxcu (Posh koo), the "baby sitter." When the five were awakened by the choking smoke, Paxcu called the children and sprang toward the plank door. Just as soon as she opened the door, she felt the searing blast from an antiquated shotgun. Twenty-one lead birdshot pellets tore into her face and neck. Paxcu slumped to the ground, but only for a moment. She knew if she remained, the long knives would be next. By sheer willpower, she staggered to her feet, and, escaping her attackers who were unable to grasp her naked body, she fled into the cornfield. The children, however, did not escape. Only Abelina survived, and only by the narrowest of margins. †

What was done in secret, soon became public knowledge. Wycliffe Associates learned about this tragedy through a letter from translator Ken Jacobs. Part of Ken's letter was published in the *Newsletter:*

> Over forty Chamulas have been driven from their homes. They're sleeping in every available space in our one-bedroom house. One family is in the corn bin; another in the wheat bin. We're running out of food.

---

† For the full story of Abelina and Paxcu, see *Night of the Long Knives* by Hugh Steven. Available through the WBT Book Room.

The Chamula believers are being persecuted
by other Chamulas who oppose their new faith
in Christ. One night a group of men set fire to
the thatch roof of a Christian family, killing
three children and seriously injuring two
others, including a young woman named Paxcu
(Posh-koo).

To help provide food for the displaced believers, the
WA administration allotted three hundred dollars and
then in October 1969, Paxcu and Abelina came to the
United States to take part in a WA banquet series. Few
who met them will ever forget their charm and deep
commitment to Christ.

A year later, the WA membership was challenged yet
again. This time the call for help came from a dot of a
village deep in the Ecuadorian jungle called Tiwaeno.
Actually Tiwaeno was a six-hundred-foot grass airstrip
adjacent to a primitive jungle settlement beside the
Tiwaeno River that had been built by Auca (now
known as Waorani) Christians who wanted to end their
isolation and meet regularly to listen to God's Carving
(God's Word) and follow "Jesus' trail to heaven."

While the name Tiwaeno wasn't exactly a household
word, even among the evangelical world, three of its
inhabitants were. Rachel Saint, Dayuma and Betty
Elliot (Betty wasn't living there at this time) captured
center stage before the world during the difficult days of
January 1956 when it was learned that five young
missionary men had been speared to death by the Auca
Indians they were trying to reach. As months passed,
God raised the consciousness of evangelicals to the
need of reaching ethnic minorities for Christ. Betty
Elliot, wife of the slain missionary Jim Elliot, wrote her
book, *Through Gates of Splendor.* Later Wycliffe author

Ethel Wallis wrote *The Dayuma Story*. Both became best-sellers and did much to challenge a generation of young people to reevaluate their careers in light of world mission.

With the passage of time and a great chorus of prayer, news broke on Easter Sunday 1960, that God had reached into the lives of the Aucas, including some of the very men who had killed the five missionaries. Later at a celebrated baptismal, the children of Nate Saint (Katy and Steve), were baptized in the same waters surrounding that same beach where Kimo, one of the Auca men, had participated in the spearing of the five missionaries. This was truly a remarkable example of God's love, forgiveness and reconciliation in action.

Then in September and October of 1969, nine years later, word came that a severe polio epidemic had struck and killed sixteen Aucas in three villages. Eleven deaths occurred in Tiwaeno. JAARS pilots immediately flew in supplies, vaccines and shuttled patients to the HCJB mission hospital at Shell Mera.

Wycliffe Associates also responded to this need. Their January 1970 *Newsletter* called for two volunteer nurses who would go on an emergency mission to Ecuador and give intensive care to the Auca polio victims. Margaret Brothers, an attractive dark-haired nurse from Pasadena, California, then working at the City of Hope Hospital, sensed God wanted her to respond. There were, however, three major obstacles— money for the air fare, a visa and time off from her work. She shared her burden with Faith Mercado, then of the Pasadena Christian Center.

For many years, Faith's father, Dr. V.C. Kelford, conducted a morning radio ministry and read letters with special prayer needs. After Dr. Kelford read Margaret's letter telling of her desire to help the Aucas,

God spoke to a Pasadena housewife who then hand-delivered a five-hundred-dollar check directly to Faith. This clear confirmation assured Margaret she should go to Ecuador, but she still needed a visa. On her first day off she went to secure her visa only to discover the government visa offices were closed. Wondering what to do next, she noticed a light burning in the Ecuadorian Consulate office and decided to knock on the door. When a man answered, Margaret explained her situation and he responded by issuing her a visa on the spot.

Margaret had the money, her visa, and her co-nurses' willingness to double up on her work load, but her supervisor offered no guarantee that her job would be waiting for her if she insisted on going to Ecuador. Nevertheless, Margaret decided to trust God for her job. On New Year's Day 1970, just one month after she had read the *WA Newsletter,* Margaret Brothers was on her way to Ecuador to an obscure village alongside a lonely jungle airstrip to help a people that most of the world considered naked jungle savages, and she was doing it for Christ's sake.

There were others, like Wycliffe nurse Lois Pederson and Rachel Saint who gave round-the-clock care to the stricken Aucas. For a moment, the situation turned even more critical than expected when Rachel came down with polio symptoms herself. Fortunately, the attack was mild and she continued on in Tiwaeno through the epidemic caring for those affected by the disease.

Further help came from WA board member and physiotherapist Ellsworth "Bud" Swanson from Santa Ana, California. He took a month off from his practice to give therapy to each of the polio victims. Bud also spent time determining the extent the ravages of the disease and developed an ongoing rehabilitation program. This involved building therapy equipment from local materials and rigging systems whereby those who suffered permanent muscle damage could exercise from their native hammocks.

Those handicapped in the jungle experience a double tragedy, particularly those who must sustain themselves by hunting and gathering. Jungle trails are largely uneven ribbons of clearing that lead through soggy marshland, swamp, under and over fallen trees, across rivers, and up sides of rough hills tangled tightly with vine and foliage. To negotiate these trails and live in such an environment requires a person's full dexterity, energy and physical prowess. They are most unforgiving of those who must be confined to crutches or a wheelchair.

The old Auca system understood this and eliminated such people by taking them to the jungle and letting them die. But now, for the first time in their history, the non-Christian Aucas were witnessing an unselfish demonstration of love and caring that was heretofore completely outside their understanding or experience. Here were foreigners giving sacrificially of themselves. So, too, were other Aucas (Christians), caring and gathering food and cooking for those stricken. No one buried sick Indians alive or threw live children into their dead parent's graves, as was the old custom. Such demonstrable love was to have a profound effect on the lives of the nonbelieving Aucas.

When Bud Swanson returned, he reported that this tragedy had forced many Aucas to face the twentieth century and to prepare themselves for the eventual inroads of outside influence. Said Bud, "There are nine Aucas who are crippled. Some have learned to cut hair, others have discovered they can make blowgun darts and exchange these for food and services. It appears that God in his usual way is accomplishing his purposes even in the midst of severe circumstances."

As for Margaret Brothers, "She had a hard, difficult job, but her contribution was priceless. She literally breathed life back into one woman she cared for. She sends her love and thanks to all Associates who prayed and shared in order that she could minister to the Aucas in their desperate need."

Another group of willing people wanted to add mission to their lives. Many of their contemporaries, however, were urging them to indulge themselves and take that long-awaited vacation. "After all," they said, "isn't this what retirement is all about?" Some retirees discovered, however, that unless they were involved in some meaningful activity, their lives became painfully empty. Said one man, "After I retired, I suddenly felt abandoned, as if I had been put on the shelf and no longer needed. Life had lost its significance." In a society where its people define their identity by deeds, to do nothing or to be isolated from that society can spell disaster or even death. Wrote one author, "The best way to have a long, happy life is to find a second career after retirement."

In most cases, retirees who choose to serve with WA are motivated by obedience to serve God and from the joy that comes from knowing one is making a useful and necessary contribution to life and the Kingdom of God. Pastor John Gaardsmoe was one of these.

For many years John Gaardsmoe pastored the largest Lutheran Church in Grand Forks, North Dakota. He had been a faithful steward of his time and energy and when the time came to retire, he did so graciously and moved to his lakefront home in Upper Michigan. But after a few months of fishing and puttering, Pastor Gaardsmoe realized he wanted more meaningful activity. He had developed a deep interest in Wycliffe after meeting Dr. Dick Pitman in Grand Forks when Dick was Director of the North Dakota SIL. Therefore, when a Chicago inner-city Lutheran church asked if he would consider coming out of retirement, and at the same time asked if he would begin a Chicago WA Chapter, Pastor Gaardsmoe said, yes!

Life in the inner city of Chicago wasn't at all like the tranquil lakefront home in Upper Michigan, but his days were full and rich. Pastor Gaardsmoe and Wycliffe translator Dr. Randy Speirs made a special tour of Lutheran colleges where Randy challenged the students to consider Bible translation as a career. And as a special project, Pastor Gaardsmoe's WA Chapter organized a fund-raising campaign to provide Randy with a new VW van.

And so it began, slowly at first, and then scores of men and women came out of retirement to offer their special skills and spiritual discernment for jobs that ranged from proofreading, to secretarial work, to gardening, to acting as housemothers, cooks, librarians, mail room workers, bookkeepers, accountants and more— all were responding to Peter's words in 1 Peter 4:10: "Each one should use whatever gift he has received to serve others, faithfully administering God's grace in its various forms." Here again WA (and WBT, too) provided the vehicle through which people could begin a totally new experience by adding mission to their lives.

Chapter Four

The Faith Promise

Once upon a time, in a little country called the Shire in Middle Earth, there lived a hobbit called Frodo Baggins. . . . Such is the setting of J.R.R. Tolkien's *Lord of the Rings,* an epic tale of wonderful heroes, of elves, dwarves and orcs, of good overcoming evil. And all this high adventure takes place in Middle Earth, a wondrous place of extraordinary aliveness, where by hard work, vision and diligence, almost anything good can happen.

During the early seventies, Wycliffe Associates was a little like Middle Earth. Its leadership and staff experienced a new vitality and optimism where, by hard work, vision, prayer and diligence, good things could and did happen. One of those "good things" happened on May 15, 1971, when the board and staff (now twenty), with the mayor of Orange and a large group of friends and well-wishers, participated in a groundbreaking dedication for WA's new office headquarters building.

The diligence, hard work, and vision required to find the right property and money to purchase it came primarily from the WA board members and particularly treasurer Rey Johnson. Said Rey of God's guidance, "I believe divine guidance comes to those who carefully and prayerfully evaluate circumstances in the light of God's Word, and then act in a positive way, trusting

God to open and close doors before you as you step out in faith."

One New Year's Eve seven months later, WA staff and friends met at 202 South Prospect in Orange, California, to celebrate the completion of their new office facilities. Many recalled the fishbowl conditions at the WBT office in Santa Ana. With every new WA staff member, desks were moved closer and closer together. The bookkeeper and *Newsletter* editor shared the same six-by-ten alcove squeezed between two full-sized desks, two chairs and two typing tables. Electric cords from an adding machine and two typewriters were plugged into a multiple outlet and were knocked out at least once a day.

Rey and Margie Johnson had become convinced that the ground swell of interest in WA's program would be hindered if the cramped, overcrowded conditions at WA on North Broadway in Santa Ana were not alleviated. Thus they launched a building project by inviting several potential donors to a dinner party to hear and meet Bill and Bettie Butler (Bill was now president of WA) and Johnny Mitchell, WA's Southwest Regional Representative, and his wife Marjorie (Mitzi). Both couples and a twelve-member staff had just completed a successful series of rallies across the U.S. featuring Rachel Saint, Dayuma and three Aucas—Dawa, Kimo and Gikita—who had participated in the killing of five missionaries.

The dinner guests listened with rapt attention as the Butlers and Mitchells recreated the high excitement of the Bible translation story via a seven-projector, multimedia presentation, operated by Wayne Cline, head of WA's audio-visual department. This same program had been presented to two thousand five hundred people in such places as the State Fair Music Hall in Dallas, and the Municipal Auditorium Music Hall in Kansas City. "And to heighten what people had seen on the screen," said Bill, "we then presented—live from Ecuador—Rachel Saint and the Aucas."

If there was a certain hawker ring to Bill's presentation, it was motivated by the noble ideal of informing the greatest number possible about what he considered the most important of mission activities, namely, Bible translation. And however one-sided that may have appeared to the Johnsons' dinner guests, one couple at least, Harold and Juanita Leasure, wholeheartedly agreed and offered to do what they could to help. Almost overnight Harold, who operated his own construction company, became the construction supervisor for the new WA office bulding in the city of Orange. (Harold would later become WA's first Vice-President for Construction.)

Bill Butler's New Year's Eve report highlighted some of the amazing ways God had worked during the planning and construction of the new office building. He thanked God for men like Rey Johnson who personally financed the property adjacent to Orange Covenant Church and for other board members who raised most of the money for the construction costs. He reminded the people how Rey Johnson, Paul Von Tobel and others had prayed that the City Planning Commission would allow them to construct an office building in a residential area. They did, without any deliberation!

And then Bill spoke about Harold's special contribution. "We have a first-class building at a third less cost than the quality of the construction would indicate," said Bill. "And the reason for this is Harold Leasure.

With his know-how and expertise in the construction industry, Harold was able to negotiate the subcontracts to our advantage. Harold also donated hundreds of hours of his own time and kept careful watch over all aspects of the construction. This allowed us to maintain high-quality workmanship, and to finish in record time. His contribution is worth more than we could ever have paid him."

Enhanced by the new office facilities, WA's "aliveness" of the early seventies came from both new projects and new people. Mary Cates had gained invaluable experience as a secretary first to Dale Kietzman in Brazil then to WBT's Executive Vice President, Dr. Ben Elson, and also to Corporation Secretary, Dr. Phil Grossman. When Mary was asked to consider joining WA's staff, she felt God would have her use her skills with WA and joined their staff in late 1970. She headed WA's editorial and publications department from 1976 until 1987 when she became Prayer Ministries Director.

In July 1971, Roger and Barbara Petrey filled a great need in the growing mail department. Roger, a twenty-five-year aeronautical engineer at North American Rockwell, had worked his way up to project manager for the Apollo Space Project, which was concerned with landing a man on the moon. At a WA promotional meeting, Johnny Mitchell challenged the people to "do something for the Lord." Impressed, the Petreys visited the headquarters. After learning WA communicates primarily through its mailings, Roger and Barbara felt God would have them join the WA staff as full-time workers in the mail-room ministry. After sixteen years of service, the Petreys have seen the *Newsletter* mailings increase from a few hundred when they joined, to forty-four thousand as of this writing. This translates into two-and-a-half tons of material that requires five working days and five skilled people each month. In addition, Roger and Barbara oversee several special mailings each year, as well as the handling and mailing of over forty thousand books sent out as part of WA's membership benefits.

Another couple to join WA in the seventies came from San Diego—Jack and Dorothy Kendall. Jack had been an energetic supporter of Wycliffe Bible Translators ever since he met Uncle Cam in 1958. From Uncle Cam, Jack learned of Wycliffe's need for technical assistance (SIL had just recently begun their Yarinacocha center in Peru). For over twenty years, Jack had worked for the Bell Telephone System and received specialized training in construction, electrical installation and personnel training. In short, he was just the man to develop and implement new water, electrical and telephone (WET) systems for Wycliffe centers.

After he accepted Uncle Cam's invitation to go to the SIL center in Yarinacocha, Peru, for a firsthand evaluation of their needs for a WET system, Jack was "hooked for life." "My wife Dorothy and I were never the same again." Jack became convinced that for Wycliffe workers to live in good health and accomplish their God-given tasks as efficiently as possible, they needed three things. One, a source of clean water. This often necessitated extensive and difficult well-digging. Second, electricity. Without electricity, a worker's efficiency dropped by half. A translation took twice as long to complete. And third, telephones. Where no telephone communication was available, particularly at a large SIL center, a good third of a worker's time was consumed in locating people to convey general and specific information. After seven trips to Peru, Jack almost single-handedly installed the first complete WET system at the Yarinacocha SIL center. In that same year (1970), with work

under way at Lomalinda (SIL center in Colombia),
Jack was assisted by a new supervisor, Wes Syverson.

Wes, a builder who came from Minnesota with
his wife, Mary Ann, had taken the SIL course in
Norman, Oklahoma, in 1968. After joining WBT, Wes
was asked to postpone taking a field assignment in
order to build a house in Waxhaw, North Carolina, for
Wycliffe's founder, William Cameron Townsend.
Although eager to begin his overseas assignment, Wes
stifled his disappointment and spent a full year building
Uncle Cam's house—alone. Actually, Wes wasn't en-
tirely alone. Each mid-morning and afternoon, Uncle
Cam came with hot coffee, rolls and conversation.
Years later Wes reflected, "When I learned I had to
spend a year working alone, I was terribly upset. I had
just come out of the construction industry where there
was always someone around to talk to or help with the
work. Furthermore, I had joined Wycliffe to go overseas,
not to spend time in the States. In my disappointment,
however, I hadn't taken into account that perhaps this
was what God wanted me to do."

For Wes, that year turned out to be one of the most
important and blessed experiences of his career. Each
morning and afternoon he had the opportunity of a
lifetime to talk one-on-one with this remarkable man—
perhaps one of the world's greatest mission statesmen.
Said Wes, "I learned a great deal about Wycliffe, its
history and its practices, but more importantly, I learned
how to relate to people in a new way. As I worked with
the subcontractors, Uncle Cam also became involved (I
had not known then that from the beginning of his time
in Guatemala, he had had an interest in construction).†

---

† See *A Thousand Trails,* by Hugh Steven (Langley, B.C.: Credo,
1984).

From those encounters with the subcontractors and others, I observed how Uncle Cam always seemed to put relationships and sensitivity to people above his own personal work or time. To this day, that special sensitivity to people and their needs, and the whole idea of building relationships, is part of my own ministry and that of the WA construction ministry.

"Many people believe that the heart of the construction and utilities ministry is to make the translator family's daily living conditions more bearable while in their allocation or on a translation center. And that is true. But it is only part of our ministry. Our men are dedicated professionals, trained to handle a wide variety of operations that include such things as providing a good source of electrical power to well-constructed housing and translation centers, and power to keep the translators' computers operating.

"We are also concerned with the emotional as well as the physical well-being of Wycliffe workers," said Wes. "We know an efficient telephone system cuts down stress. Without a proper communications system, a translator has to continually jump up and run between buildings and houses to communicate. Of course, the clean water drilling project under project manager Dave Beaty is self-explanatory. We are excited about the way the wells have speeded up translation by freeing up the time a translator has to spend hauling and sterilizing water. We are also excited with the way a clean, pure water system can serve the whole community.

"In one village in Peru, the disease rate dropped seventy-five percent when the people began using pure well water instead of muddy lake water. Providing a clean, pure water system for the translator and the community in which he or she works shows our concern for the physical as well as the spiritual well-being of the people we serve. Foreign governments appreciate this and allow our translators more freedom to do their work.

"But as important as all this is, the lesson I learned from Uncle Cam during the year I spent building his house was that the ministry we have to the volunteers who help us is probably as important as the work we accomplish for the missionaries. That's the first thing I tell our volunteers. Any building we build or any phone system we install might last ten, fifteen or twenty years. But what we do for the Lord will have eternal rewards.

"Incidentally, this is one reason why we like to use volunteers over paid professionals. First, of course, there is a tremendous cost savings. But more importantly, the volunteer usually has a burden for missions and while a paid professional can do a good job, the volunteer will give above and beyond what a paid professional will often do."

After twelve years in South America, Wes and Mary Ann returned to the United States where Wes assumed the directorship of WA's worldwide WET ministries. Jack Kendall's last major project, and the one he said was the culmination of his dreams, was the supervision of telephone systems at four widely separated SIL centers in Brazil. Author Jim Hefley wrote about this mammoth undertaking in his book *God's Free-Lancers*. But since this project embodies the essence of WA's total ministries, it bears repeating.

Said Jack, "It took just twenty-six days for a team of WA communications specialists to install a dial telephone system in all four centers." To which Jack's wife, Dorothy, said, "The miracle of this time difference doesn't register until one remembers that it took Jack nearly seven years to install the same type of system at the Yarinacocha center in Peru. What a difference teamwork makes!"

In 1972, another significant couple joined WA's growing team. John and Liz Bender went to Brazil to serve as WA missionaries. John had served on a construction work party in Central America and later decided to give up his construction business. Like Wes, John would return after years on the field to the U.S. and assume the directorship of WA's Construction Ministries at the WA office in Orange, following Harold Leasure's time of service.

Standing behind these men on the field were Joe Girard and his wife, Mickey, on loan to WA from WBT. Amazingly, it was Joe who, a few years earlier, had challenged Bill Butler to consider Wycliffe as a place of service. Now here he was serving as the Coordinator of WA Field Projects, directing the movement of volunteer workers and equipment. Joe's job was one of logistics that grew more complex every month.

Continuing with its response to needs within WBT, WA asked several of its board members to take a short field assignment to Jungle Camp (then held in Southern Mexico, but now called Americas Field Training Course [AFTC] and held in Southern Texas) and speak to Wycliffe members-in-training about how they might better relate to their supporting churches and friends. (This predated WBT's successful furlough workshops and reentry seminars.)

One of the first to accept this challenge was insurance broker Paul Robbins and his attractive and enthusiastic wife Virginia (Jinx). Both Paul and Jinx were Wheaton College graduates and had a number of former college friends in Wycliffe. A few months after Paul joined the WA board, he and Jinx were ploughing their way up a jungle river in a narrow dugout canoe to speak to a group of Wycliffe trainees.

Paul and Jinx gave the new recruits a series of informal seminars (similar to those given in the WBT furlough workshops) on personal grooming and how to give an effective presentation of their individual slides and other visual materials. They encouraged an honest presentation not only of their joys and successes but also their sorrows and failures. And when Paul and Jinx returned home, they echoed what many had said before them and what hundreds have said since. "It was a privilege to be a part of this project. We will never be the same again."

By WA's fifth anniversary in 1972, membership stood at six thousand. Construction teams were building hangars, translation workshop facilities and clinics in such diverse locations as Peru, Colombia and Brazil. Following one step behind were the WET teams and a Canadian Wycliffe Associates ministry formed under Wycliffe's Canadian Home Division and headed by Nelson Weston.

To keep the home constituency more informed about WBT's and WA's expanding ministry, Dale Kietzman narrated a daily five-minute radio program over twenty-six radio stations. "Translation Report" featured current reports from various Wycliffe fields. Additionally, hundreds of Associates had responded to participate in the WA Hospitality Roster. This practical expression of love for the many Wycliffe churches, family and friends instantly became a two-way blessing.

Wrote one couple who opened their home to a Wycliffe worker, "Of all the many outside influences upon our children, none can compare in impact and blessing with having a Wycliffe missionary in our home." Ken and Judy Greenlee, charter WA members from California, opened their home and through Wycliffe workers Don and Annabell Weber, felt God's call to join Wycliffe as translators. Today the Greenlees serve the Endo people in Kenya's Kerio Valley.

Not all who opened their homes became "full-time" Wycliffe workers, although Will and Marsha Pritchard from Plantation, Florida, who lodged hundreds of Wycliffe workers, must have felt they were indeed in "full-time" service. Besides playing host, the Pritchards established a vigorous WA chapter in Fort Lauderdale, and coordinated several large WA banquets.

In 1972, the centerpiece of this "aliveness" was the Faith Promise Banquets. What had begun with two banquets in 1968 had grown to five hundred eighty-seven with an aggregate attendance of one hundred fifty thousand. From these, twenty-one percent had committed themselves to a faith promise. (In 1972 alone, WA conducted two hundred eighty-eight banquets in thirty-eight states with an attendance of eighty-six thousand three hundred forty-eight).

For many, the notion of a faith promise was a new innovation in Christian stewardship. Some were puzzled by it and wondered if giving to WA on behalf of Wycliffe reduced giving to their local church. Dr. Oswald Smith's famous film, *How God Taught Me to Give*, presented the faith promise principle superbly. But for those who hadn't seen the film, Dale Kietzman put the faith promise principle into a biblical and historical perspective saying, "The faith promise has been used to support missionary outreach for at least one hundred years. It apparently was initiated by A.B. Simpson in his missionary conferences in the 1880s and was the basis for the early growth of the Christian and Missionary Alliance world missions."

When the late A.W. Tozer was asked about the origin of the faith promise plan, he said, "As far as I know, the idea originated with Dr. Simpson. Of course, Simpson thought it originated with the Apostle Paul. Basically, a faith promise is a commitment made to God based *not* on how much money one has, but on how much money you believe God will provide, which money you, as God's steward, can give directly and purposefully to his work in the world. A faith promise is income one would not normally expect to receive—or additional income to be supplied as a result of faith and prayer.

"The focus of the faith promise is to encourage every Christian to exercise his faith in fulfilling God's desire for his Church and the world. Motivating people to trust God is a duty and a privilege. Thus a faith promise teaches Christians to develop the muscle of faith. A faith promise then is based not on your known resources, but on faith in what your Heavenly Father will do. It is promising to give to his work what you believe God is going to supply. [However, one can also make a faith pledge from his or her known income.]

"It must be remembered that a faith promise or pledge is not made in fleshly confidence, but in trust in the gracious, giving God Who gives to those who expect miracles. But it is a promise made for the keeping, and it certainly would include the element of personal sacrifice. God forbid that we should even think of giving something that cost nothing. And yet, could we think of making a promise that we would take no responsibility for keeping? It takes faith to make a faith promise; and it takes integrity to keep it."

Having integrity and developing empathetic sensitivity to need applies to the Wycliffe worker as well as to his supporter. WA's business manager Doug Meland, along with his wife Doris, WA's graphic artist in the seventies, had worked for ten years among the Fulnio people in northeastern Brazil. Among the Melands' friends was a local government official, Sr. Coriolano

Mendonca.

The Melands had maintained a faithful witness to the Mendonca family and while there was polite attention given to what Doug and Doris said, no one in the family had made a firm commitment to Christ. When Sr. Mendonca learned that the Melands were going to leave Brazil for another assignment in the United States, he assured Doug that he would become a Christian before they left. But no commitment was made. The Melands left without Sr. Mendonca indicating his intention to follow Christ.

Then one day the Melands received an urgent letter from Sr. Mendonca with the tragic news that his eldest son Sebastian, a recent medical school graduate, had lost his left arm in an automobile accident. Without an arm, the young man's medical career would end. When Doug received this news, however, he realized that more was at stake than simply the loss of a career. Now the Fulnio people, living in one of the poorest areas of Brazil, would be denied the medical care Sebastian was planning to supply.

Knowing that Dr. Sebastian Mendonca was unable to provide an artificial arm for himself, Doug presented this need to WA constituents through the *Newsletter*, then to several hospitals and an airline. Amazingly, all three responded. A Brazilian airline provided a free ticket to the United States where Sebastian could undergo therapy and be fitted with an artificial arm. The arm was paid for through gifts from the hospital staff and donations from WA members. Said Doug, "Dr. Mendonca came to California and in four weeks returned to his homeland not only with a new arm, but with a clear testimony of true Christian love and discipleship."

But Dr. Mendonca wasn't the only person to receive a

prosthesis through WA's help. One night in Ecuador, Emma Lucitante, a bright fourteen-year-old Cofan girl, suddenly felt what she thought was a thorn prick in her bare leg as she walked beside tall grass along the riverbank. To her horror and the dismay of her parents, the "thorn prick" was the lethal fangs of a poisonous snake.

Within several days, complications from loss of blood and a too-tight tourniquet turned Emma's leg numb and black. After five days of "treatment" by a village shaman, Emma's father knew his daughter would die if she didn't get outside help. Loading her into his dugout canoe, he traveled several hours down-river to a developing oil town. But for all his pleading, no one could help.

Resigned that his daughter would die, he started to return home. As he was about to leave, a JAARS pilot landed at the oil town on routine business and learned of the Cofan girl's need for medical treatment. Immediately, the pilot offered to take Emma and her father to the SIL center at Limoncocha. The father accepted. After a blood transfusion, antibiotics and other medication, Emma still needed more extensive treatment than even the well-stocked clinic at Limoncocha could offer. She was then flown to the HCJB hospital at Shell Mera. After the doctor examined Emma, he said sadly that the only way he could save her life was to amputate her lower right leg.

That happened in 1968. In 1972, Jim Olsen, working in Ecuador with a WA work party from California, met Emma through Bub and Bobbi Borman, translators for the Cofan people. During their visit, Jim noticed that Emma wore long, red stockings.

"Aren't long stockings too hot to wear here in the jungle?" asked Jim.

The Bormans then explained about Emma's snake-bite and her artificial leg. "In fact," said Bub, "since Emma is still growing, this is only a provisional leg and it's causing her trouble. We will have to think seriously very soon about getting her fitted with a permanent leg."

"Emma is an amazing young woman," continued Bub. "She's a natural-born teacher. Along with flannel-graphs of Paul's journeys, she's taken our translation of Acts to her own Cofan people and has introduced several to the Lord."

So touched was Jim Olsen by Emma's story that when he returned to California, he, together with Dan Doyle, then Wycliffe's Miami office manager, began making arrangements to have Emma fitted for a new artificial leg at an orthopedic clinic. And, just as it had been for Dr. Mendonca, Emma's air fare, hospital expenses and money for a new leg were all provided by concerned and empathetic Wycliffe Associates.

In May 1974, in appreciation for all she had received, Emma, then aged nineteen and a bilingual school-teacher, wrote an open letter of appreciation to WA. The letter also told of how awestruck she was when she left Ecuador and saw the ocean for the first time.

"I was overcome by its immensity," she wrote. "I thought about Jesus and how He really is Owner of all." After relating how she finally got her "rotten leg cut off," Emma wrote, "I got well but I walked only with great effort. But then some people came, and a lot of people began to pray to God, and I came to the United States where I received a new leg. Now I have forgotten how sad I was. With my new leg I can walk better. I pray that God will repay all of you for having helped me.

"When I went to Limoncocha they told me about Christ. At first I didn't understand what they told me.

But after I heard a lot, I understood and believed. Now knowing God I want to live without fear. I want to tell all my relatives about God. I don't want to ever stop living for Christ. This is all I write, Emma."

Most Wycliffe Associates, like Jim Olsen, and Paul and Lois Eby of Fort Lauderdale, with whom Emma stayed during her stateside convalescence, respond to need out of true Christian compassion—a compassion that translates into action and says, "Seeing a need, I do what I can to help in a concrete way, because in helping people, I thereby show my love for God" (see Hebrews 6:10b).

And so, through the mid-decade of the seventies, Wycliffe Associates responded to needs with the exuberance of an adolescent in spring who has discarded his winter boots for a new pair of tennis shoes. From Daly City, California, came a donated twenty-three-foot fire truck for the SIL center in Colombia. WA construction crews consisting of aircraft mechanics, bookkeepers and doctors, worked as one, hauling gravel, mixing cement and driving nails to build new translation study facilities in Peru, Colombia and Brazil. In almost every case, when the people returned after their two weeks or month or however long they had committed themselves to a work crew, they told how they had received much more than they had given. They had enjoyed fellowship, been given a new vision for missions and had the joy of giving to people who truly appreciated their help.

But then in January 1975, WA experienced a dramatic shift in leadership. After seven years as its president and co-founder, Bill Butler gave up his presidency to assume the leadership of another organization, Christian Resource Management.

This was a serious blow to WA's entire operations

because with Bill went about thirty-one of WA's office staff. Overnight the vitality that had characterized WA's beginning years gave way to a more serious analysis of their future. The most immediate need was for an interim president and new office staff to keep the momentum going. The man chosen for this task was charter member and chairman of the 1975 WA Board of Trustees Rey Johnson. Serving as chief administrator to oversee the WA office and implement new programs was Executive Vice-President Doug Meland. Together, both men and the WA staff took the promise of Deuteronomy 31:8 (NAS) as their rallying point: "And the Lord is the one who goes ahead of you; He will not fail you or forsake you. Do not fear, or be dismayed."

Despite this reorganizational change, 1975 became a year of continued growth and expanded ministry. Arthur Greenleaf III in the Northeast and Gary Chaffin in the North Central area were added as area directors. These two, with Stan Shaw in the Southwest, and Paul Chappell in the Southeast, carried out WA's work throughout the U.S. Dave Houston was Vice-President for Public Relations, Warren Nelson was Program Director, and Bob Fischer acted as Extension Director.

When Cyclone Tracy severely damaged the SIL center in Australia, WA members responded dramatically to this and other emergencies. And then with a new year and a new spirit—the spirit of '76—WA's leadership resolved under God to make Wycliffe Associates one of the world's most effective Christian organizations. Their resolve was to involve more of God's people in the great unfinished task of the Church. Their enthusiastic resolve, however, would need more time to mature.

Chapter Five

A Pause for
New Direction

He will call upon me, and I will answer him; I
will be with him in trouble; I will deliver him
and honor him (Psalm 91:15).

In mid-March 1975, concerned family, friends and
colleagues learned that John and Carolyn Miller
and their five-year-old daughter LuAnne, plus six
others, had been "detained" by Vietnam's Liberation
Armed Forces. One of the comforting promises from
Scripture that sustained the Millers during their eight
harrowing months of captivity was the above verse.
(This had been given to John as an "anniversary gift"
while holed up in the U.S. government compound in
Banmethuot, just hours before their capture.†)

From the beginning, Wycliffe Associates had shown
a special interest in SIL personnel working in Vietnam.
The *Newsletter* often carried feature stories and special
calls to prayer for their safety and progress. In August
1971, the feature cover photo and story was of the
Millers' Streamline Imperial Mobile Coach being
loaded aboard a ship bound for Vietnam. After the 1968

---

† See *Captured* by Carolyn Paine Miller. Available through the
WBT Book Room.

Tet Offensive, the Millers were forced to adopt a seminomadic lifestyle to be with and minister to the Bru people, for whom they were translating the New Testament. Like thousands of others, the Bru were innocent victims of war and had become refugees within their own country. Touched by the Millers' obvious lack of self-interest and their willingness to remain in an extremely difficult situation for Christ's sake, WA and others helped finance the cost and shipping of the trailer.

In May 1973, the *Newsletter* carried one of its most poignant stories. Evangeline Blood and her four children appeared on the front cover with the caption, "A Letter to Cindy." It was from the Wycliffe family and began:

> Dear Cindy:
>   Hank Blood is more to you than just a name in the news report. He was your dad, and Wycliffe's only prisoner of war in Vietnam. In these days when you are experiencing the heartaches of knowing your father will not come home, a lot of people are thinking of you . . . ."

Hank Blood had been taken captive along with Betty Olsen, a Christian and Missionary Alliance missionary and Mike Benge, a USAID advisor after the Tet Offensive. Five months later, suffering from pneumonia and malnutition, Hank died. † Now, in May 1975, the *Newsletter* once again brought the injustice and pain of war to the attention of those who would pray for the Millers. In a single caption of a full-page photo of John

---

† See *No Time for Tombstones* by James and Marty Hefley (Wheaton: Tyndale, 1974).

and Carolyn, the Wycliffe constituency was confronted with the possibility of yet another Wycliffe casualty. It read, "All Wycliffe Personnel Evacuated From Vietnam Except The Millers."†

These were clearly turbulent and distressing times, both for the world at large and for Wycliffe. And for the first time since its beginning in 1967, Wycliffe Associates was also experiencing its moments of agony.

While there was no ill will when Bill Butler left with thirty-one of WA's staff, those who remained—Rey Johnson, Doug and Doris Meland, Sarah Pease, Mary Cates and the Petreys—faced an enormous challenge and an uphill struggle.

The challenge was to keep the momentum going that had been generated under Bill Butler's exuberant leadership. But the period between 1975 and 1979 turned out to be a pause between what had been and what was yet to come. The skeletal WA staff and volunteers did their best to continue the programs that had been established. The banquet series continued, as did the call for involvement in special projects and the construction and WET ministries. But it was as if that certain spirit that had propelled WA into its grand strategy had paused and was marking time, waiting for the key men and women God had foreordained to assume their roles in WA's ministry.

But before this could or would happen, two of the most pivotal men in WA's history would have to take a South America trip together. In turn, these two men would influence, disciple and groom the man who would propel WA into a whole new dimension of

---

† The December 1975 *Newsletter* carried yet another full-cover photo of the Millers. This time the caption read, "Millers Home For Christmas!"

service and outreach. That man was Al Ginty—a man of great determination, vision, administrative skills, and a man with spiritual sensitivity.

The two men who, in the late 1970s, gave decisive leadership and prepared the groundwork for Al to assume his role as president were Roger Tompkins, WA's Chairman of the Board of Trustees from 1977 to 1983 (and currently WBT's U.S. Division Council Chairman), and Rev. George Munzing, Pastor of Trinity United Presbyterian Church in Santa Ana, California, and a WA board member.

The scenario of how this came about is a rich tapestry of "chance" meetings, casual bits of conversation and other "coincidences." One spring afternoon in 1975, Doug Meland, then WA's Executive Vice-President and a member of Trinity, accidentally met George Munzing in a restaurant parking lot. Doug asked George if he would be interested in leading a special ministry team to Colombia, Peru and Brazil. The object would be for the team to gain a more in-depth understanding of the stress and problems associated with missionaries who live and work cross-culturally.

A man of energy with an interest in travel and missions, George Munzing quickly agreed. Actually, the invitation couldn't have been more opportune. George was then in the middle of a sabbatical from Trinity and welcomed the opportunity to use his special pastoral gifts.

One of the first to accept George's invitation to go on this special ministry trip was Roger Tompkins, a new member of Trinity. Only months before, Roger and his wife Elinor had gone with an adult Sunday School class from Trinity to view the recently-built Wycliffe Bible Translator headquarters in Huntington Beach. The "tour guide" for that special event had been WBT's then

Executive Vice-President, Dr. Ben Elson, also a member of Trinity.

Apart from that brief introduction, Roger was unaware of Wycliffe's worldwide ministry. He, like George, however, was interested in travel and missions. A gifted business manager, Roger is regional vice-president of State Farm Insurance Companies in Southern California. He is also keenly interested in the Scriptures and is an experienced lay teacher and discipler of men. The other ministry team members included Dave Hansen, a college student and part-time youth worker at Trinity, and Trinity's then Children's Education Director, Paula Carson.

There is no way to accurately gauge the impact the team had on all those they met and ministered to. But some comments from Roger's journal give us insight into WA's claim that when Christian people give themselves in service and ministry, they receive infinitely more in blessing and reward than they give in time, effort and money.

Wrote Roger during the first week:

> We have prayed for the Lord to manifest Himself in what we do. All of us have been involved in some aspect of ministry. I am glad we came. At first it was difficult. It took time to shape and focus in on what we were about. But I believe God is shaping us as his tools to work through us and in us these next weeks.

In summing up after the trip, Roger wrote:

> Was it worth it? Without question. Not only did I enjoy the travel and sight-seeing, but I was blessed with several specific areas of ministry:

to one WBT member who was considering a new assignment in business administration but was unsure of his next move; to two SIL directors who appreciated new management concepts and practical helps for their branches; to several students and their parents in Brazil who allowed me to act as mediator and reconciler. Being a missionary's kid doesn't isolate one from teenage conflicts.

Did we all minister? Yes, we did, emphatically —to each other as team members and to each other in the Body of Christ. We did this through prayer, participation, and sharing. Although George [Munzing] was our leader, we all took leadership roles at various times with various people. The beautiful thing was that none of the ministry was in any way a "canned" presentation. Everything was spontaneous, just as the Lord led and directed us.

What are the long-range implications? I am not called to be a WBT translator on a field in some foreign country, but I am open to whatever He has for me in the future. I am deeply impressed with the commitment and tenacity of the people who are working on the field, be they translators or support personnel. What could have a more profound impact on the lives of people than giving them God's Word in their own language? I know how much the Scriptures have meant in my own life and am certain they will have the same impact in the lives of the indigenous peoples. I was impressed with the way the Spirit of God was at work in the lives of many of the Indian people I met.

I am encouraged that God continues to answer

prayer to bless individuals in order that they can bless the whole church. Time and time again we saw evidence of answered prayer in the lives of WBT people, the tribesmen and in our own lives. For my part, this trip has caused me to:

    —Extend my knowledge and understanding of the Wycliffe-SIL system.

    —Be open to the Lord as to what role, if any, He may have for me in interaction with WBT people.

    —Try to keep in contact with some of the people we met as they come home on furlough as well as by correspondence.

    —Encourage others to accept calls and opportunities to minister, should the Lord open doors, to WBT people, whoever they are.

Roger proved as good as his word and intentions. When he returned home, he immediately joined WA and was soon elected to the board. He served as WA's president from 1979 to 1981, but we are getting ahead of our story!

To understand the sequence of interlocking events, it is necessary to go back in time to a baseball park in Orange, California, between the years 1965 and 1974. For nine years, George Munzing managed Little League teams while his three sons played their way through this icon of Americana. Also managing a team was Al Ginty, who was then vice-president and general manager of the electronics division of the Anaconda Corporation. The two men learned that each had a son playing on opposing league teams and exchanged the usual ballpark pleasantries. In 1974, Al also coached the all-star team and worked with George's son Dan, one of his all-star players.

The following spring, George's wife Carol accidentally met Al in the same Little League park. She learned that Al had left Anaconda after twenty years of service. With several months' severance pay, he was enjoying his time off—playing golf, reevaluating his life and looking into a new career. When Carol told George, he phoned Al and invited him to play golf.

From that casual conversation, subsequent golf games, and fellowship, George and Al became fast friends, often discussing spiritual things. Up until this point, Al had been active in many churches, but his friendship with George channeled him into a vital personal relationship with Jesus Christ. With it came a new openness and fellowship with God and his people. Al and his wife Vivian, who had joined Trinity, began to attend an in-depth Sunday School Bible class led by Roger Tompkins. Al's interest in the Bible profoundly influenced his life. And, because they had common business interests, Al and Roger also became friends, with Roger ministering to Al as a spiritual mentor.

In the fall of 1978, Al once again left a successful business venture. During this interim, however, he had begun to sense God's call to Christian ministry. Before preparing his resume, Al prayerfully reflected on God's gifts to him and asked to be shown where his experience as a lay person could be put to the best use in ministry. Al shared this with his Bible study group at church, and two nearby Christian ministries were suggested—WA and Athletes in Action (AIA). George Munzing, his pastor, was on WA's board of trustees, and suggested he speak to WA's then president, Jim Shaner (Jim had been appointed by the board in May 1976).

Believing WA might be the Lord's direction, Al interviewed with Jim and learned he was looking for an assistant. Al accepted the position and in July 1978, the *WA Newsletter* formally introduced Al as Vice-President for Program Ministries.

When Jim Shaner and his wife Maxine joined the WA family and staff in 1976, several major projects were underway. At the beginning of his administration, Bill Butler had seen the need for a facility where Wycliffe personnel could retire with dignity. Finally, on February 15, 1976, Santa Ana Councilman Harry Yamamoto, Rey Johnson, Doug Meland, and Clarence Church, then U.S. Division director, broke ground in Santa Ana for the thirteen-story, two hundred-unit apartment complex to be called Wycliffe Plaza. Within the year, the building was completed. Among the first occupants in Wycliffe Plaza were Don and Alice Smith. Don, a retired postal employee, had served as Wycliffe Associates' first Mail Department Manager. Don continued to serve WA enthusiastically, even after the Petreys replaced him.

The Construction Ministries in 1976 focused on an airstrip in Lomalinda, Colombia, as well as the installation of a phone system at the new International Linguistics Center (ILC) in Dallas, Texas. Also, three major systems (water, electricity and telephones) were being installed at SIL centers in the Philippines. But perhaps the most significant projects in 1976 had little to do with hammers, saws, retirement centers, or faith-promise banquets. It had to do with an eleven-year-old girl, the twin daughter of Wycliffe workers Ted and Lillice Long.

Ted and Lillice worked in Peru as community development coordinators among the Shipibo people. On April 20, 1964, God gave the Longs a special gift—twin daughters whom they named Merrily Rose and Merrilyn Dawn. The birth of these two lovely children brought the Longs both joy and pain. Pain because one of the twins, Merrilyn Dawn, was born with severe congenital eye and kidney problems. Her life expectancy was two years.

After the doctors at UCLA Medical Center in Los Angeles had given Merrilyn Dawn a six-week checkup, they said simply, "All we can recommend at this point its to give your daughter a special diet and lots of love." And that's exactly what the Longs did. After two eye operations that restored partial sight to Merrilyn, plus the application of prayer, faith and love from her parents, older brother Paul and her twin sister, Merrilyn kept going on what she herself later coined as "heavenly power."

About age nine, as Merrilyn Dawn began to approach puberty, the UCLA doctors warned the Longs that her small kidneys would not be able to handle her body's growth demands. They estimated she would have to have a kidney transplant or be put on a dialysis machine within two years.

Their estimate was a year short. When Merrilyn was eleven, a Lima kidney specialist (the Longs had returned to the field) advised Ted that his daughter's kidney was deteriorating. The specialist conferred by phone with Dr. John Merrill of the Peter Brent Brigham Hospital in Boston, Mass., one of several doctors who had pioneered in kidney transplants with twins. Both doctors agreed that if Merrilyn were to live, a kidney transplant must be done as soon as possible.

When Ted Long shared this news with Merrily Rose, she flung herself across her bed in anguish and tears over what she considered the great unfairness of her sister's suffering. Of that night, Merrily said, "As I lay thinking and praying, I glanced over at Merrilyn sleeping so blissfully, unaware of what was going on.

Mom wasn't home and I wanted to talk to her so badly. The doctors at UCLA Medical Center had said that if I were eighteen, I could legally give one of my kidneys to Merrily. But I knew I couldn't wait. She wouldn't live that long. I had to give her one of my kidneys now!"

This was no knee-jerk reaction. Merrily admitted her fear. She had always been less-than-brave about getting injections or visiting the dentist. But that night the realization that her sister would die if she didn't donate one of her kidneys transcended all fear and discomfort.

Later that night when her mother returned, Merrily said, "Mom, I am going to do it."

"Do what?" asked her mother.

"I'm going to give Merrilyn one of my kidneys. Dad told me she might die if she doesn't have a transplanted kidney soon. I know God wants me to be the donor."

Lillice Long was astonished at her young daughter's pronouncement and tried to assure her that this wasn't her problem.

"No," said Merrily, "I know you and Daddy and Paul have been thinking that one of you should be the donor. But I am an identical twin, and I am the one to do it." The conversation continued the following morning. Again Merrily Rose affirmed her desire to donate her kidney. Thus began the hurried preparations of packing and making arrangements for travel to the States from Peru. In the midst of the myriad details, the Longs began to experience a deep sense of peace that all the difficulties would be resolved. Even the realization that Merrily was a minor, and they would have to go through court proceedings to secure legal permission for her to give her kidney to her sister, no longer troubled them.

High on the Longs' list of priorities was to place a radio call to Wycliffe Associates and ask for help with some of their immediate needs. Ham operators Lee and Edna Farnsworth, Associates in Santa Ana, put through a phone patch from the Longs to Doug Meland at the WA headquarters in Orange. Happily Doug agreed to notify the Longs' supporting churches in Southern California, and offered to find lodging for them in Boston.

Longtime Wycliffe friends at Park Street Church in Boston were contacted. The person who answered the phone was Betty Vetterlein, sister to translator Dow Robinson, and daughter of Grace Robinson, who had in her retirement served Wycliffe as a librarian in Huntington Beach. When Betty learned of the Longs' need, she and her husband Russell, an insurance broker, invited the Longs to stay in their home.

The Holy Spirit's assurance given before they left Peru was indeed being realized. Not only was a home provided and help from a Christian attorney to prepare their legal case, but Arthur Greenleaf, then WA's Northeast area director, introduced the Longs at a WA banquet, and told something of their situation. Afterward, a large number of people assured Ted and Lillice of their prayers, and some offered to give blood.

On October 29, 1975, Merrily Rose and Merrilyn Dawn were admitted to the Peter Brent Brigham Hospital in excellent spirits. God had given both special calm and peace. Surgery was performed the following morning at eight o'clock. Many on the hospital staff, including the receptionists, telephone operators, coffee-shop cashiers and others anxiously awaited the outcome. And when the girls came out of anesthesia, the staff and others spontaneously hugged each other.

That afternoon Lillice sent word to their families and friends. "Both girls are doing well. Kidney working fine.

Everyone has great peace. As far as we can tell, the operation is one hundred percent successful."

Recently Lillice reflected on her emotions at the time the twins were born.

My pilot husband was in Lima on business and the babies decided not to wait for him. I was alone when I received the sad news of Merrilyn Dawn's condition. She had been born with glaucoma in her right eye, a cataract on the left, plus internal problems, and since it had taken almost twenty minutes for her to begin breathing, there was possible brain damage. But in a wonderful way, God had prepared me, for I was filled with his peace and acceptance.

I remembered the Israelites' forty years of wandering because of disobedience and unbelief, and I prayed to the Lord for Him to help me not to wander around in the wilderness of self-pity and dismay. I also prayed that the Lord would help us as a family to stay on his path, and accept these babies just as they were, because that's the way He had sent them. I honestly didn't feel any depression or regret. It seemed to me that God was saying, "These children are going to be a part of your future ministry, not a hindrance to it. Just take your hands off, let Me be in control and watch Me work."

And that's exactly what has happened. God has kept his promise and overwhelmed us with his goodness as a family. Throughout the years, Merrilyn Dawn has amazed everyone with her undauntable spirit and determination to be independent. She even learned to ride a bicycle

down a jungle path to school. Before and after
surgery, the girls demonstrated a beautiful faith
in God and we believe this brought glory to our
heavenly Father.

And what happened to Merrilyn Dawn after receiving
her sister's kidney? The May 1976 *Newsletter* printed
the Longs' answer to that question that said in part, "We
expect many of you are wondering if the news is still as
good as it was right after surgery. Yes, it is. Merrilyn and
Merrily are fine. Merrilyn has gained a total of twenty
pounds and grown two inches just since December.
   "Along with a perfect operation and recuperation, we
praise the Lord for all the people He brought together to
take care of our need. Wycliffe Associates brought
people together at just the right time and we are grateful
for their logistical and financial help."
   Curiously, that same *Newsletter* ran a simple sidebar
that told of the death of Robert Bartholomew, a
longtime friend of WA and one of its founders. He had
acted as Recording Secretary before WA had an official
name. It was a poignant reminder of life's transience
and that interesting couplet, "Only one life, 'twill soon
be past, only what's done for Christ will last."

Chapter Six

Quality Programs
with New Ideas

History writers often force historical events into neat, self-contained homogenous units. However, when the major transition in WA's history occurred at the end of its first ten years and a noticeable new team spirit began to emerge at the beginning of its second decade, then one must mark this natural bridge as a critical turning point in WA's history.

The transition began when Rey Johnson assumed the role of interim president in 1975, through to Jim Shaner's presidency beginning November 1978. It would be wrong to suggest that little was happening during those years. On the contrary, several major projects were begun, like Wycliffe Gardens, the fourteen-story, one hundred eighty-five-unit retirement facility in Huntington Beach and five apartments that WA construction volunteers built for transient WBT workers and visitors at the SIL center in Guatemala City. The Mexico-Cardenas Museum at the JAARS Center in Waxhaw, North Carolina, was also built, supervised by Harold Leasure, the general contractor for the WA office building in Orange. This museum conceived by Uncle Cam provided an avenue to honor the memory of Lazaro Cardenas, Mexico's president from 1934 to

1940. It was President Cardenas's friendship with Uncle Cam that gave SIL an open door to Mexico in the 1930s.

During this time several WA staff members were also assigned different tasks and this left vacancies for new people to fill. Some, like Bill Nyman, West Coast area director, who joined the WA staff in October 1977 with his wife Marjory, brought with him years of missionary and public relations experience. His father, William G. Nyman, had been Wycliffe's first treasurer, and when it came time for Bill to consider his own calling from the Lord, it seemed a natural step for him to join Wycliffe Bible Translators.

Bill met his wife Marjory while serving in Mexico among the Zapotec people. Later Bill and Marjory served Wycliffe in a variety of public relations positions in Mexico, Peru, Venezuela, and Waxhaw, N.C. Immediately before joining WA, Bill served as chief public relations officer for SIL in Bogota, Colombia.

In 1978, a former high school teacher and band director from Rock Hill, South Carolina, joined the WA staff. Peter Brouillette, with his wife Shirley, became key players on the new team as Peter assumed duties as Southeast area director.

In celebration of WA's twentieth birthday, Al Ginty reflected on those years and wrote in part:

> Since 1978, God has richly blessed Wycliffe Associates with tremendous growth and expansion through several dynamic board members under the leadership of Chairman Roger Tompkins, who served as WA president from 1979 to 1981, after Jim Shaner.
>
> Roger, an experienced Bible teacher, brought to WA a wealth of business skills, Christian

leadership, and team management that helped give WA a broader vision.

With new directions for lay ministry, the combined talents of the WA board, the larger and more highly trained staff, and better organized programs, WA provided broader opportunities for even more lay involvement.

A new dimension of WA member service and financial strength was sought during this period to allow the organization to draw through the resources of a larger, more informed membership.

This not only funded the WA ministries and key Wycliffe projects, but allowed more lay people to claim the promise of Matthew 10:41: "Those who serve or support a missionary because he is a missionary will receive a missionary's reward" (paraphrase).

Among the energetic board members was Pastor George Munzing, whom God used to channel several of his church members (including Finance Vice President Dave Crawford and me) to the WA staff during 1978-80.

Paul Von Tobel III (whose father Paul II also served on the WA board), Ernie Warner, Roy Long, Charles Stillings, and Billy Gibson added strong direction to the board team.

Board member Bob Seng's spiritual depth and active leadership in the Tucson Chapter, was a great witness and strength to this group of lay people with its strong desire to see Wycliffe fulfill the great goal of reaching three thousand-plus unwritten languages.

Lloyd Bontrager was a driving force who generously shared his resources and Christian commitment, and Margie Johnson was a strong influence with her vision for a WA prayer ministry.

Over the years, other board members such as Glenn Larson, Lin Erickson, Lucille Sollenberger, Chet Bitterman, Ruth Hoyt, George Ferrone, Clarence Shaw, Mose Gingerich, Otto Janke, Nathan Bruckhart, Harm te Velde, Elroy Condit, Homer Kandel, Roger Brownson, Ken Wilcox, and others, representing all sections of the U.S., made major contributions of time, skills, and money.

So, under this strong board leadership, WA's second ten years of ministry was launched, energized, and supported.

Rapid growth and positive membership response to this new team spirit eventually lessened the constant struggle to pay the bills so that quality programs could be developed to build an effective ministry for lay people.

With Wycliffe Bible Translators experiencing a great surge in members, a plethora of new Wycliffe projects and needs were undertaken by WA in South and Central America, Asia, North America, the Pacific, Europe, and Africa to bless lay people and allow them to be a blessing.

Resources developed by WA for Bible translation were increased from $721,000 in 1979 to $3,573,000 in 1985. And resources totaling $16,704,000 were raised during this challenging seven-year period when God was opening new doors for translation all over the world. . . .

This spendid report, for obvious reasons, passed over the strategic planning necessary to create these astonishing banquet statistics, "Two hundred eighty banquets each year in four hundred thirty locations in the U.S. every eighteen months." Astonishing because when Al assumed the responsibility for banquets under his title, Vice President for Program Ministries, the banquets were floundering.

It wasn't that the faith promise banquet concept failed. The banquets were still the most effective vehicle WA had for introducing new people to Wycliffe's mandate of Bible translation. Part of the "floundering" resulted from unworkable internal monetary arrangements between WA and WBT. WA also needed a larger vision for lay involvement through the banquets and a better-trained back-up organization to "make it happen."

When Roger Tompkins became WA's board chairman in May 1977, he was faced with deficit spending. WA had committed itself to several important projects, without money to implement new programs.

Serving on the board with Roger was his pastor and friend, George Munzing, a man whom God gifted to ask insightful and often penetrating questions. He was thus able to immediately get to the core of tangled and complicated issues. Both he and George could justifiably claim Mordecai's words to Esther, "Who knows but that you have come to this position for such a time as this?" (Esther 4:14b).

It was also in May 1977, that the WA board met in Mexico City concurrently with the WBT and SIL international conference. While there, Roger and George learned that several WBT executives held WA's banquets in disfavor. Some believed WA's format did not represent WBT's true nature and purpose.

On the return flight from Mexico City to Los Angeles, Roger and George discussed this and WA's limited funds. Jokingly George said, "It looks like I'm to serve on the board of an organization that you've been elected to chair and it might well go under in a year."

Yet, despite this, the WA board (Roger and George in particular) had caught the vision of WA's original intent. Namely, to provide programs and services for lay people to become involved directly with Bible translation. They resolved that night to work hard and creatively to keep WA's mandate alive.

These noble ideals alone, however, would not revitalize the faith promise banquets. At this critical moment, God allowed Al Ginty, then responsible for Banquet Ministries, to become part of the solution.

The *Newsletter* writeup officially introducing Al and Vivian said that Al had joined WA at an appropriate time, a time when new goals for growth were being planned. No statement about Al could have been more true. Uniquely, Al had gained just enough experience under the old banquet format to give him a better vision of what was needed for a more modern program.

Although Al honored WA's founding principles, he did not refrain from suggesting fundamental changes in approach. Said Al, "We need new and refreshing ways to hear about God's work. The challenge before us is to make the banquets and other related WA programs meaningful enough to encourage more lay people to make some kind of commitment."

The strategy for the banquet revitalization, and later the expanded WA ministries, originated from fundamental principles Al learned many years before. "To further any enterprise," said Al, "one needs good fellowship and teamwork."

True teamwork, of course, involves *esprit de corps*, an inspiring enthusiasm that directs everyone's efforts toward desired results. WA was born out of such a desire. Said Al, "When you get the proper mix of lay people and missionaries together, exercising their God-given gifts, things can really happen."

One of the first things that happened was the recruitment of qualified Wycliffe speakers from the field who were trained to present their material in a pleasing, well-thought-out, logical and exciting manner. The man responsible for this initial training program was Claude Bowen.

Considered one of America's best storytellers, Claude had for many years directed the Dale Carnegie Institute in Chicago. A dedicated Christian and Wycliffe enthusiast, Claude, through the friendship of the then U.S. Division Director Clarence Church, offered fifty percent of his time to train WBT personnel in public relations and public speaking, including speakers for the WA banquets. (The Townsend Institute for International Relations, held at Wheaton College each summer, is an outgrowth of Claude Bowen's ministry to WBT.)

Al Ginty also urged his area directors to train for this professional excellence. At previous banquets the speakers often didn't synchronize their message with the theme of the banquet. Often several elements of the program were unplanned until the last moment.

Perhaps Claude's greatest contribution was his insistence that speakers present only firsthand experiences, and be told as stories in short, two-minute modules. From years of training top management and from his own reading of Jesus' parables, Claude knew people respond more enthusiastically to stories than a recital of facts. To tell a story as Jesus did is to engage the mind as well as the heart. It captures the listener's imagination and can become the vehicle through which the Holy Spirit can touch a person to become involved in world missions.

In order to eliminate unrehearsed programs and the perfunctory meeting of the principal speaker and master of ceremonies just hours before the first banquet meeting, Claude had them, and others who had a part in the banquet program, take part in a five-day seminar. Here he lectured, told stories and introduced storytelling techniques, giving each speaker professional guidance in preparation and presentations. Likewise, the emcees learned how to move quickly through their programs with grace and facility.

Somewhere, swirling just below the consciousness of those who wanted to bring a new professionalism and maturity to the WA banquets, was the need to demonstrate a new understanding of the Gospel and its implications for the seventies and beyond. Here were people who wanted to combine both faith and technology to bring about commitment, but they wanted this always to be held in balance. In the beginning, this balance was not always observed, and Al began to implement his own special dictum: "We must put on quality programs at the lowest possible cost."

This program streamlining was just the beginning. Said Al, "If we want people to respond to our ideas and to move them a notch closer to mission, we must concentrate on the basics. We must appeal to their senses as well as remind them of the mandates from Scripture."

For Al, as program director, the basics included well-groomed, appealing speakers. Claude Bowen allowed no discussion on what he considered well-groomed male speakers and emcees: conservative dark blue or black suit, white shirt with a dark tie, and polished black shoes. One newly-recruited master of ceremonies wearing a maroon jacket with brass buttons, a checkered tie, matching checkered pants and brown shoes, received a quick, no-nonsense rejection from Claude!

Appetizing food, of course, was another basic to be

served in an attractive, comfortable setting conducive to good fellowship. Confirming these basics, Al says, "Laymen speak and often think differently from the professional pastor or missionary, and we in WA are committed to addressing ourselves to the interests of laymen."

Al's sensitivity to laymen grew from his experiences of staying in their homes. From casual conversations, Al learned what people liked and didn't like about WA. Some banquet reservation secretaries, for example, felt overwhelmed by their tasks. In every case, Al made notes and tried to find a solution to the problem. One solution was to share this burden with a larger local committee. And to avoid clashes between highly motivated, single-minded WBT workers and more laid-back Associates, Al and his staff functioned as arbitrators and liaisons.

Central to the development of professionalism (not to be confused with slick presentations), was Al's desire that his staff also match WBT's image—excellence in mission achievement and commitment to people. His commitment to teamwork, and his oft-repeated dictum, "You can't get anywhere without first building a team," applied not just to WA at large, but also to his office staff. He knew that their involvement in management decisions would make them a more productive and happier staff. One indispensable staff member then and now is his wife Vivian. Possessed with an amazing memory, and interpersonal sensitivity, Vivian often shared with Al many comments and suggestions from donors' notes as she processed WA member responses, faith promises and other donations. From these, Al received important feedback on WA programs.

Following Jim Shaner's resignation, Roger Tompkins

served as both WA's chairman of the board and
president from 1979 to 1981. He remained, however,
regional vice-president of Southern California's State
Farm Insurance Companies. While he met with WA
staff one morning each week, he left day-to-day staff
operations to Al Ginty.

In the spring of 1979, George Munzing represented
WA at WBT's biennial conference. One critical item on
the U.S. Division agenda was whether or not to continue
WA's charter as an organization. In that meeting,
George carried the day with his strong, convincing
logic. "Under Al and Roger's wise, steady leadership,"
he said, "the area directors have been stabilized and
there is a sense of corporate history being established
that gives a new consistency and stability to the
programs that are being implemented."

When George completed his report and reaffirmed
WA's role as a servant to WBT, the agenda item about
its future never came up for discussion. "It was clearly a
watershed experience," said Roger later, "and from that
day forward, WA has hardly looked back."

Chapter Seven

Golden Jubilee

Consecrate the fiftieth year and proclaim liberty throughout the land and to all its inhabitants. It shall be a jubilee for you (Leviticus 25:10).

Perhaps the most striking feature about WA's second decade has been its openness to new ideas, new possibilities and a new willingness to act creatively within the framework of its servant mandate. This openness has worked in concert with the Holy Spirit's desire to bring about a community of people who are motivated by the basic bonds of Christian love and a desire to be part of God's timeless purposes. As a result, they are keenly aware of their "neighbors" and want to give away God's love that has been freely given to them.

Rey and Margie Johnson, like so many other Associates, have spent the past twenty years of their lives sharing this "indebtedness" through practical leadership. While serving on WA's board from 1978 to 1982, Margie introduced several important and innovative programs. One was the Aunts and Uncles Program begun in 1980.

During a trip to South America with other Associates, Margie sensed the uncertainty and fear of several Wycliffe young people planning to return to the U.S. for college. Faye Donmoyer, a pretty teenager with honey-blonde, shoulder-length hair, shares her fears, memories and anxieties about leaving her home in Peru in this written prayer:

Dear God,
Today I was thinking about leaving home and my family. I thought of all my memories of Yarinacocha as a little girl—the picnics, playing in the rain, climbing trees, catching bugs, campouts, making forts, running barefoot, all the games we played, skinned knees, bicycle riding, canoeing, roller-skating, junior high, swimming in the lake, cycle rides, my pets (dog, parrots, honey bears, monkeys, opossums), struggling with schoolwork, taking care of animals, screened windows, my plants and orchids, piano lessons, informal church meetings, young people's retreats, all my friends. . . .
Lord, I'm going to miss this place, too. It's beautiful—palm trees, flowers, full moons over the lake, sunrises and sunsets, animals, mosquitoes, crickets and frogs chirping, rain on the roof, citrus trees, cycles, sunshine, and loving and caring "aunts" and "uncles". . . .
I feel kind of like Peter, Lord. I'm stepping out in faith. I'm trusting You to meet my needs. Lead me. Help me keep my eyes on You because that's the only way I can get anywhere. And Lord, teach me to number my days to make each one count and spend it as I should. Help me as I enter college and face new experiences.
Thank You for all those people who are praying for me, Lord. Bless them.

Some months after her trip, Margie spoke with a

Wycliffe couple visiting their son in college. Again she heard the apprehension and pain of separation when they said, "The hardest thing we've had to face is knowing our son is so terribly lonely. Because he didn't know anyone, he spent the important holidays alone in his room."

With three teenage daughters of her own, Margie empathized with parents and young people caught up in this unhappy circumstance. As she prayed and thought about the problem, she remembered that children on the field often referred to Wycliffe adults as aunts and uncles. Therefore, she reasoned, why not have the same relationship for WBT young people in the States? Said Margie, "The trauma of leaving home, of being separated from parents and friends, could be eased greatly by a loving family who would offer support and encouragement. There must be many Wycliffe Associates who, if they knew about this need, would open their homes and be delighted to act as a substitute aunt or uncle."

Dave and Billie Slade, a husband and wife team, volunteered their time to coordinate the Aunts and Uncles Program, matching Wycliffe young people with Christian families who live near their schools and jobs. Currently this program is supervised by Kevin Lincoln, Administrator of Missionary Services at the WA office in Orange.

Margie's second innovation occurred just as her term on the WA board expired. For years she had realized that many hundreds of Associates wanted a more active role, yet could not physically enter into the overseas work programs, construction ministries or banquet series. Margie envisioned their role as a great untapped resource for prayer. When she left the WA board, she passed on her burden to incoming board member

Lucille Sollenberger. By 1984, this seedling idea blossomed into one of WA's major ministries.

Moving into the eighties, it was a little like Janus, the ancient Roman statue who had two faces, one young and one old. WA's young face eagerly pressed toward the future. But there was also the old face. It represented the many Associates who had gone to be with the Lord. Bill Wyatt and Jack Kendall were two of these. Both had given themselves skillfully to WA's early direction, and both were involved with WA right to the end of their lives in 1979. Actually it would be more correct to say "right to the beginning of their lives," because for the true believer in Jesus Christ, death is the beginning of life—eternal life. Both men could now claim Paul's words, "Death is swallowed up, and victory is complete!" (1 Corinthians 15:55a, Barclay).

Paul also has a word for those called to remain "by the stuff." "Therefore my dear brothers [and sisters], stand firm and immovable. Work always for the Lord to the limit and beyond it in the certain knowledge that the Lord will never allow all your toil to go for nothing" (1 Corinthians 15:58, Barclay).

The beginning of the eighties also marked the time when Al Ginty was officially oppointed as WA's Executive Vice-President. In 1980 Dave Crawford, now Vice-President for Finance and Personnel and Assistant Treasurer, joined the WA staff. John Bender, now a Vice-President, was appointed Director of Construction. Also in 1980, Bernie May, former JAARS Executive Director, replaced Clarence Church as Wycliffe's U.S. Division Director. This is an important post for WA since both WBT and WA directors work closely with one another. Much of WA's direction for program priorities and Wycliffe's project needs come through WBT's U.S. Division. In the early eighties, three special projects that came one on top of another so challenged and stretched WA's corporate faith that WA was never to be the same organization again.

The first project was building Wycliffe's new "Jungle Camp" facility, now called Americas Field Training Course (AFTC), in Uvalde, Texas. Relocating "Jungle Camp" to a scrub brush and cactus ranch eighty miles west of San Antonio was precipitated by the growing political unrest in its former location in southern Mexico. The man most responsible for the lion's share of detail planning and building this important training facility was WA's new Director of Construction Ministries, John Bender.

Before joining WA, John ran his own construction company in his hometown of Hartville, Ohio. One day a friend challenged him to use his skills for volunteer mission outreach. John accepted the challenge and made five trips to Guatemala. Some time later, he and his wife Liz became part of a work party to Ecuador. Said John, "It was there that the Lord got hold of my life and sold me on Wycliffe workers, and when I saw firsthand how translation was carried out, I was challenged with a new perspective for my life. I thought, if translators and support workers can live a life of faith, why not carpenters?"

Why not indeed! When John and Liz returned from Ecuador, they contacted WA and were challenged once again. Wes Syverson, who had been working in South America, invited them to join the construction and WET team. "In this way," said Wes, "you'll multiply your talents."

That was in 1972. Six years later in December 1978, after working on major construction projects in Brazil, Colombia, and other countries in Latin America, John returned to the WA office in Orange to assume directorship of WA's construction ministries.

John was sold on the concept of partnership, of involving lay people in a hands-on mission experience. Often in the past, when he had needed extra volunteers, he had few "buddies" he could call on, and most often he could count on one or two or several to volunteer a week or two on a project. But the Uvalde project needed more people than John had immediately at his disposal. Under the heading, "Help Build Wycliffe's New Jungle Camp," John wrote the following article for the May/June issue of the 1980 *Newsletter:*

> WA is going to build Wycliffe's new Jungle Camp in southern Texas! Since relocating from Mexico, Jungle Camp is now known as Americas Field Training Course (AFTC). If you have basic carpentry skills and some free time this summer . . . read on.
>
> *When?*   This summer during July and August.
>
> *Where?*   El Rancho de Agape, ten miles east of Uvalde, south of Highway 90. (Uvalde is eighty miles west of San Antonio.)
>
> *What?*   A large kitchen/dining/meeting hall and thirty small, simple cabins.
>
> *Why?*   Facilities must be ready this fall.
>
> *Who?*   YOU! . . . if you have basic skills and a few basic tools. Contractors and skilled workers, too. Builders, how about bringing your crew for a few days?
>
> And bring your family! There'll be a job for everyone. We'll need volunteers to cook, and care for the

small children. Some teenagers can help at the construction site.

WA will have a project supervisor there at all times to direct activities and work.

How long? Come for as long as you can.

Facilities: Bring your own camping equipment—tents, campers, motorhomes. Electricity and portable toilets provided. A cook/mess tent, run by AFTC staff members, will provide meals at cost for those unable to cook.

Travel: You must provide your own travel. If you fly in, we'll pick you up at the airport. If you fly your own plane, make arrangements directly with the Uvalde Municipal Airport (runways lighted at night).

Fellowship: We anticipate good fellowship, singing, sharing, and testimony times around campfires . . . volleyball and swimming, too, and all-day trips to Mexico each month.

Purpose: AFTC trains Wycliffe's young recruits in jungle living and survival to prepare them for remote areas. In a few years they'll be translating the Scriptures in many countries, and we'll have helped get them there!

You'll receive terrific blessings by your on-the-scene involvement. You'll fellowship with AFTC staff members and get a deeper look at

> Wycliffe's work. . . . and you'll enjoy
> meeting other Associates from all
> over. Best of all, you'll be serving the
> Lord as you help further Bible
> translation.

Following this announcement, a short sidebar told
the amazing part Lloyd and Glenda Brown, owners of
the El Rancho de Agape, played in this important
project.

> El Rancho de Agape is bordered on one side
> by the spring-fed Frio River. On its twenty-three
> hundred acres, dotted with scrub brush and
> cactus, cattle share the wide open spaces with
> white-tailed deer, jackrabbits, and armadillos.
> It's a ranch with a purpose. Owners Lloyd
> and Glenda Brown, although active in their
> community and interdenominational fellowship
> group, One in Christ, Inc., wanted to do more.
> So they bought the ranch to use for God's
> purposes—a camp. . . a school. . . .
> In March when Glenda met AFTC staff
> members Tom Salisbury and Bev Brander in
> Uvalde, she learned of Wycliffe's need for a
> permanent AFTC site. Said Lloyd, "When I had
> lunch with Glenda that day, I could see she was
> really excited. She was trying to figure out a way
> for the Wycliffe people to come immediately.
> Then I met Ron Snell, the course director and,
> after he told me what they're doing, I really
> wanted to help with their work."
> Lloyd and Glenda offered the use of their
> land . . . and gave fifty thousand dollars for
> materials to begin the project! What generosity!

... and what an encouragement to all of us!

And they'll have their school, too. They're building an accelerated Christian day school that's already swamped with applicants.

The Browns believe in sharing the resources God has given them. We're grateful for such enthusiastic, committed Christians and for their great gift to Wycliffe's ministry.

John's article, couched in language of highest optimism, actually launched into a great unknown. "This project," said John, "was a pure step of faith for the WA Construction Ministries and myself. Never before had we invited volunteers to participate in a major project in the continental United States. Many people respond to work parties because they want to have an overseas experience, but would people come to Texas in the hottest part of the year?"

John was absolutely correct about the heat. Uvalde was then in the midst of the worst heat wave on record with temperatures reaching a searing one hundred ten degrees. Further, this was the first time anyone had been invited to a project that hadn't any of the usual amenities. For those sleeping in tents, the only shower facility was a garden hose hung over a pole, and the "kitchen" was a couple of stoves set under a piece of canvas stretched between two poles.

John superintended the construction job himself, leaving his desk work and coordination of other work crews around the world in the capable hands of his secretary, Wendy Steven. As the July 4 commencement date drew closer, John had no idea who or how many people would come. Said John, "With all of these so-called negatives working against the project, I couldn't blame anyone for not coming."

But people did come. Eighty-eight in all. Some, like professional roofer Joe Adair, flew his own twin-engine Cessna 320 and brought a crew of five. Wayne West pulled a trailer all the way from Southern California. Within nine weeks, this remarkable team, including several young people and children, built twenty-seven small cabins and one large multi-purpose building.

Said John, "I can't remember a group of people who were more committed and bonded together in what they were doing. We had a wonderful time of fellowship. In fact, so rich was this fellowship and sense of purpose that few wanted to leave when their two-week vacations were over. Some phoned their employers and asked for extensions. Most of the employers thought these people must be vacationing on some lush, tropical island. Few believed anyone in their right mind would elect to spend their precious vacation time on some remote Texas ranch in one hundred-degree heat without air conditioning, showers and proper eating and sleeping facilities. On the surface, it may have seemed strange, but not for those who had experienced the fellowship, the rich camaraderie of people committed to a single purpose and sense of mission. They had caught the vision that by building these facilities that would one day house hundreds of Bible translator trainees, they themselves were actually participating in Bible translation."

Meanwhile, under John's leadership, other WA volunteers were at work in a variety of places around the world. One crew of five who went to the Philippines reflected the multicultural and geographical divergence of WA volunteers. From Calgary, Alberta, Canada, came Adam and Maxine Martin; from La Habra, California, Chet Niles; from Boulder, Colorado, Greg Anderson; from South Dakota, Lonnie Waldner.

John supervised, adding to his previous experience in Central and South America. This crew renovated and expanded Wycliffe's crowded study and living facilities in Manila. As in all projects, they faced their share of frustrations and problems. "We constantly had to improvise," said Lonnie, "because materials weren't easily available." But when the crew accomplished in three weeks what would have taken the translators six months to a year, minor frustrations and problems paled into insignificance. Additionally, WA volunteers worked in Peru, Bolivia, Suriname and Australia. And while Al and John thanked God for what was happening, they also realized WA staff and resources were being stretched to their limits.

Like all living substances, WA was an organism that wanted to preserve its existence. Its openness to new ideas and possibilities gave Al, his staff and the WA board the freedom to dream, to see the whole, rather than just the parts. Therefore, when WA was further challenged in 1980 with the unique opportunity to become the sponsoring agent and help raise funds and provide the logistics for Wycliffe's Golden Jubilee in 1981, they accepted.

The idea for a jubilee celebration came first from Ethel Wallis, co-author of *Two Thousand Tongues to Go* and author of *The Dayuma Story,* as well as other Wycliffe books and articles. Ethel, a longtime Wycliffe translator and friend of Uncle Cam, wanted to, in some way, commemorate the fifty-year anniversary of the dedication in Guatemala of Cameron Townsend's translation of the Cakchiquel New Testament.

At first this notion seemed beyond WA's capabilities and experience. Wisely, Al Ginty sought outside help. A successful Golden Jubilee would require a team effort —a joint venture with the U.S. Division and the good will of Wycliffe's many friends and supporters. At first, U.S. Director Bernie May hesitated, believing this celebration might confuse the Wycliffe constituency. WBT's fiftieth anniversary as an organization would be in 1984. However, as the initial enthusiasm gained momentum, he lent his support to the project.

An early supporter of the project enlisted by Ethel Wallis was WA board member and nephew of Uncle Cam, Lorin Griset. Lorin had considerable experience as a chief coordinator for the Southern California Billy Graham Crusade in 1964. He chaired a steering committee that later became the Golden Jubilee Committee and was co-chaired by Bob Welch, a WA board member.

One of the WA board's major contributions to the Jubilee was to give this event its initial direction and purpose. They wanted to make this more than just a celebration in honor of Uncle Cam's fifty years of Bible translation. Said the board, "Let's use this celebration as a major promotion to accelerate recruitment of Wycliffe missionaries."

In the fall of 1980, the Year of Jubilee began. Appropriately, WA made the Jubilee the centerpiece for three hundred fall banquets all across the United States. The September *Newsletter* advertised this event and told about a great public celebration that would take place in the Anaheim Convention Center in Southern California on May 9, 1981. If the Jubilee was to promote recruitment, as co-chairman Lorin Griset suggested, then WA had the responsibility to promote this theme and provide a channel through which the church and local communities could be informed and challenged through the banquet format.

Therefore, on February 17, 1981, in the Anaheim Convention Center, pastors and church leaders from over two hundred congregations in Southern California were invited to a special "pastors" luncheon. Speakers for that event were U.S. Division Director Bernie May, Rachel Saint, George Cowan, Manuel Arenas and the powerful Argentinean evangelist Luis Palau. Luis Palau challenged the church leaders to trust God for four hundred new Bible translators and support workers during the Jubilee year. Many who attended the luncheon said they left with an expanded vision of mission and a new sense of responsibility to help spread the Gospel to the world's hidden peoples.

The luncheon proved to be a splendid prelude to the large May 9 public celebration. In readiness for that celebration, Otis Skillings, director of the Skyline Chorale, was commissioned to compose an appropriate anthem. Billy Graham agreed to be the principal speaker, accompanied by Bev Shea and Grady Wilson. Uncle Cam Townsend was to be featured in a "This is Your Life" segment along with his wife Elaine and their four children. Dr. Ken Pike, his wife, Evelyn, and Rev. Donn Moomaw of Bel Air Presbyterian Church would also participate and the emcee was to be the articulate Al Sanders.

In the midst of all this high excitement was one sad unknown. On January 19, 1981, seven political activists burst into the SIL guest house in Bogota, Colombia, and took captive a young Bible translator. For the next seven weeks, Wycliffe constituents prayed for the protection and release of this husband and father of two daughters. In the providence of God, however, Chet Bitterman was not released. His body was found March 7, wrapped in a guerrilla flag. He had been drugged and shot by his captors.†

---

† See *Called to Die* by Steve Estes (Grand Rapids, Mich.: Zondervan Press, 1986).

As in times past, the martyrdom of a saint has been used by God to awaken others. On May 9, Chet's young wife Brenda and the Bitterman family joined the many special guests on stage in the Anaheim Convention Center. In response to the Spirit of God speaking through Billy Graham, Uncle Cam and others, one hundred nine young people made a commitment to become part of the Bible translation ministry and "take Chet's place."

Later, as Al Ginty reflected on the Golden Jubilee he said, "The Lord truly brought together a brand-new combination of people, events and circumstances that profoundly affected and expanded not only WBT, but also WA's ministry. In 1980, one hundred seventeen new workers were accepted into Wycliffe. After the Jubilee in 1981, that number almost doubled to two hundred nine. A year later, in 1982, WBT accepted two hundred fifty-one new recruits. I know it's difficult to accurately measure the effects of one's programs, but we believe the public awareness of the Jubilee, the banquets, TV programs and all the other media events, plus the personal contacts and WBT books, were all used by God to bring the needs of Bible translation to the attention of dedicated Christian young people."

While WA's leadership appreciated the rise in WBT's enrollment, Al realized that the significance of the Jubilee went far beyond just a recruitment "event." Said Al, "The Jubilee taught us all something about the nature and development of ourselves as an organization. At first we went into the project with fear, dragging our heels. But through the experience, God opened our eyes, enlarged our vision and increased our faith to tackle other projects that prior to the Jubilee would have overwhelmed us. In a new way, God surprised us far beyond our expectations and we saw the great difference a team makes when each one pools his or her gifts and talents."

These were not just emotional words spoken after a sudden burst of optimism. Rather, they were carefully measured, filled with reality, because at the moment Al was reflecting on WA's greater capacity to serve. John Bender and his construction crews were already planning to build a sixteen-unit, two-story motel plus a twenty-eight suite, two-story apartment at WBT's Huntington Beach headquarters. Both would greatly alleviate the critical housing need for those assigned to this high-cost area.

Al and Vivian Ginty also remember 1981 as the year Roger Tompkins, who had served as WA's interim president since 1978, relinquished his presidential duties. Al, who had served as Executive Vice-President for almost two years, was appointed WA's President.

Together, Al Ginty and Roger Tompkins reviewed WA's activity for 1981 in the annual report. After the 1978 "crisis" when Roger and George Munzing both wondered if WA would survive, the report reflected an absolute miracle of God on WA's behalf:

> We have every reason to praise God for the tremendous blessings and growth he poured out on WA throughout this Jubilee Year. Since Wycliffe Associates is lay people in action, it's a pleasure to highlight those who participated in Wycliffe's Bible translation ministry through WA programs and services.
>
> Nineteen eighty-one was an excellent year. It exceeded our expectations and allowed WA's resources for Wycliffe Bible Translators to increase fifty-two percent over 1980, from $1.1 million to $1.7 million. This includes banquet

projects, construction, missionary support, recruiting services, special projects, and *Newsletter* projects.

This report features several projects and programs WA accomplished this year. Of special interest are:

The GOLDEN JUBILEE special project at the Anaheim Convention Center in Anaheim, California, in May with Uncle Cam Townsend, Billy Graham, Brenda Bitterman, and six thousand enthusiastic people. This project focused on Wycliffe's recruiting needs. It also provided emphasis to several other WA activities and brought resounding response from lay people throughout the country.

Luis Palau set the keynote that challenged churches to provide the needed Bible translators and support workers. Jubilee project results are expected to continue throughout the eighties.

CONSTRUCTION more than doubled in 1981. Three hundred twenty-two lay people (up eighty-four percent) volunteered and paid their own travel expenses to provide over five hundred fifty thousand dollars' value in construction of facilities at Wycliffe centers.

The HUANUCO TRANSLATION CENTER in the Peruvian Andes attracted seventy-five lay people to build facilities to speed translation for over two million Quechua Indians.

The COLOMBIA TRANSLATION/STUDY FACILITY at Lomalinda was a heartwarming project that allowed our lay people to support the brave missionary team in Colombia during the difficult period after Chet Bitterman's death.

The BANQUET program had a fine year of

growth. This year's attendance was thirty-three thousand four hundred forty-nine for two hundred banquets. Faith promises increased twenty-four percent to nearly five thousand for major projects in Latin America, Indonesia, Malaysia, and the Philippines. As part of the Golden Jubilee Year, a recruiting theme was featured with encouraging results. WA banquets continue to be the leading edge for all WA ministries.

The TUCSON PROJECT brought fast and amazing response of housing, prayer support, working facilities, fellowship, and encouragement to over fifty translators stranded in the U.S. and exiled without visas from their Mexico tribes.

Wycliffe Associates completes its fourteenth year with a membership of nearly twelve thousand. WA ministries are coordinated by twenty-seven full-time staff people, including five U.S. area directors and two construction supervisors, with direct involvement by scores of volunteers. Most staff people work at WA headquarters in Orange, California, the central link between our lay Associates and worldwide Wycliffe (WBT/SIL) operations.

Our personnel include a few WA veterans whom God has blended with several new young people working as a team in a busy, productive atmosphere. Training seminars regularly upgrade skills. WA staff are encouraged to trust God for spiritual and professional growth. As committed Christians, they strive to combine fundamental ministry skills with a "heart for missions."

WA revenues for 1981 were $1,848,000 compared with disbursements of $1,794,000. This produced a surplus of $54,000 for additional ministry. Number of gifts increased sixty-five percent in the past two years. Added to this growth, the Lord has blessed WA with over twenty-two thousand giving partners and with operating facilities that are free from long-term debt. WA has adopted Wycliffe's fiscal year-end change to September 30, and our financial statements reflect a nine-month year (for 1981 only).

Looking to next year and on ahead, we see many new opportunities and great needs for lay people in Bible translation. Major projects in Kenya, Chile, Peru, Huntington Beach, Cameroon, and Ethiopia are being planned or are under way. Growth of current WA programs is needed to keep pace. To assure this growth, as well as the emergency of new areas of productive lay ministry, the WA board established a Long-Range Planning and Program Policy Committee.

During 1982, WA will expand its construction ministry to local lay groups and churches. We've witnessed rich blessings and new life in a church or community that sponsors a group of lay people for a WA construction project in fellowship with a trained WA field supervisor.

Although Wycliffe suffered setbacks in Mexico, Panama, and Ecuador, persecution in Guatemala, difficulties in Asia, and martyrdom in Colombia, it was a great year of progress. During the past two years, nearly fifty New Testaments were completed. Bountiful harvest from Summer Institute of Linguistics training sessions indicate that four hundred fifty people from the U.S. alone will join WBT/SIL this year, an increase of over forty percent. The challenge also is great to redeploy to Africa, Asia, and other vital areas the hundreds of Wycliffe missionaries completing their work in Latin America during the eighties. The facilities and services needed to support this growth and relocation will be massive.

In the past year, the Lord has reinforced WA's vision of active lay people as the essential growth element in mission work. We're privileged to send you this full report of WA's operations with detailed financial statements. Net resources are directed to Wycliffe's evangelical work of Bible translation.

We praise God and dedicate this report, with sincere appreciation, to Wycliffe Bible Translators, the WA Board of Trustees, our staff, and to you, a lay person in action.

Chapter Eight

Ministry Through Construction and Hospitality

Those who live in southwest Arizona, especially the Tucson area, don't need to be sold on the truth of the statement, "It's a great place to live." They are surrounded with the harsh beauty of towering chimney mountains and rocks and cliffs that stand guard over a vast landscape of mesquite, scrub brush and the famous giant saguaro cactus. It's a landscape that seems to be forever changing color. Sometimes muted greys, sometimes blanketed in vivid greens; other times light pink to deep rust, or hazy blues to purples. And in the midst of all this natural beauty and wonder, a quiet wonder of another kind has changed the landscape.

In September 1982, on a forty-acre site at the base of the Santa Catalina Mountains, about twelve miles north of Tucson, WA volunteers and others from Disciples, Inc., began to build a translation center for Wycliffe personnel who could no longer live and work in Mexico. Some distance from this center, these volunteers and others also built several houses for Wycliffe workers, the first permanent homes many had known since joining Wycliffe.

Then in rapid succession came a six thousand-square-foot, two-story building with space for a library and thirty study cubicles. A temporary administration building followed, (as of this writing this functions as the center's technical-studies building). Completed in 1986 was a large U-shaped building for the administration, post office and auditorium.

The husband and wife team most responsible for responding to the Mexico Branch's need for a permanent work place, housing and retirement site is Bob and Betty Seng of WA's Tucson Chapter. When Bob, who had served six years as Vice Chairman of WA's Board of Trustees, was asked to comment on his involvement with WA and what this long-term commitment has meant to him and Betty, he said:

> When WA began in 1967, I saw in this organization the opportunity to become more deeply involved in nontraditional ways. As a believer in Jesus Christ, I appreciated my salvation and felt a general concern that others also come to know the Lord. The traditional method for lay people to help in missions is to pray, give dollars and listen to the missionaries when they come home. This is great and necessary. But I wanted a way to become more personally involved, and I wanted to do it right away!
>
> My wife and I run a small insurance company in Tucson and I didn't have the time to fill out long application forms or spend years in Bible school or seminary to meet the requirements for overseas service. WA's ministry allowed me the opportunity of going out immediately, but more importantly, WA offered me a ministry of exercising my own practical skills in a meaningful and helpful way. It was this that stimulated me to become involved.

After forming a WA chapter in Tucson and participating in various WA-related projects, Bob was challenged in 1975 to go to northern Mexico and help convert an old stable into suitable living accommodations for Ron and Sharon Stoltzfus, translators to the Guarojio people. Said Bob:

> When I learned about this translator who, with his pregnant wife and young daughter, was trying to make over a mud-roofed and dirt-floor stable into suitable living quarters, I said to the men of our Chapter, "Let's go and help. Let's commit ourselves to this need." God just seemed to remind me, "There are a few of us men who can go down and build this in a month, whereas Ron will be at it for a year or more!"

As Bob presented this need, he wondered if his motivation was simply the romance of going to a foreign country. To make certain this was God's will and not just his own desire, he put out a fleece and asked the Lord to meet four conditions. To make it absolutely foolproof, Bob decided not to tell anyone of his prayer request. To his own amazement, each condition was met. They included a specific dollar amount for the project, the number of men who would actually go, approval both from the then Mexico Director John Alsop, and the approval of his wife Betty who would bear the heavy business responsibility during his absence.

> As I look back, I remember that it was a tremendous struggle for me to leave my business. It was small and needed daily care and oversight. Up until that time, the only vacations I took

were long weekends. In some ways, it almost appeared irresponsible for me to be taking off on this project. Yet, I knew it was the right thing to do. In a strange way, I felt I was being yoked with the Lord. He said, "Take my yoke upon you," and I felt I was doing exactly what He wanted me to do. Throughout the three-week building project in Mexico, I experienced a new sense of God's presence and joy.

Bob experienced other benefits from that first project as well. A bothersome skin ailment cleared, and surprisingly, for the first time, he wound up his year-end accounts on time. And he gave all the credit to the Lord for doing exceedingly abundantly above what he had asked.

When the Mexico Branch needed to expand the translation center with retirement housing and mobile-home sites, Bob and the Tucson Chapter were ready to trust God and take an even greater step of faith. Through a remarkable series of events, Bob and several other WA members secured an additional eighty acres at about half the going rate. This saving they passed on to the Wycliffe membership. Said Bob:

The rest is history. When the word got out through the *WA Newsletter* that we needed help to build missionary housing, people came from all over the United States and Canada. It would be unfair to say that I was the only one responsible for this center because so many have helped. All of this has been the Lord's doing. He brought a great team together; Betty and I were just the catalysts. It's as if the Lord said, "If I had chosen someone with more money and experience, they wouldn't have had to trust me. It would not have been a work of faith." And the exciting thing about the Tucson project was that it was exactly that—a work of faith!

One volunteer who served on the Tucson project was Ric Winter. In 1981, Ric, with his wife Carol and their four children, lived in Lake Tahoe, California, where he ran his own construction company. One evening at a Wycliffe meeting, Ric met John Bender and for the first time saw the film, *Mountain of Light.*

Said Ric, "I'd read *National Geographic* and seen documentaries on many Third World countries, but when I saw how these particular people in Papua New Guinea lived and died, I was deeply moved. Moved because I came to the startling conclusion that I had been giving most of my strength and attention to my own tiny little world. When I admitted this to myself, the Lord spoke to my heart and said, 'There are other worlds you know nothing about.' "

In the morning, after a fitful night, the Spirit of God led Ric to read Ecclesiastes 12:1: "Remember your creator in the days of your *youth* . . . ." Once again the Lord spoke to his heart. "For the next forty years you will exhaust yourself working to maintain an extravagant lifestyle, spending more than you earn, and when you have grown too old to hold a hammer, you will come to me and say, 'Use me.' "

Convicted, Ric said simply, "God, I want you to use me now. I want to give you the best days of my life—the strongest days of my life."

At John Bender's request, Ric and two of his employees agreed to spend a week working on the Tucson center administration building. On the flight down from Reno, one of the men questioned Ric about who would be there to help them.

"There will be some volunteers," said Ric.

"Volunteers? What kind of volunteers?" asked the other man. "Are they familiar with construction?"

"No," said Ric, "I don't think so. One's a mailman, two are farmers and another is an airline pilot."

The two men expressed their incomprehension by the traditional furrowed brow. "I have no idea what we'll find," said Ric, "or how it will work out. All I know is that God wants us to go, and we're going."

What they did experience was unbelievable. In just one week, these so-called "unskilled" volunteers laid a two thousand-square-foot cement slab, framed the building, shingled the roof, installed windows and almost all the plumbing. (Ric and his team were to insulate and hang and tape the drywall.) Said Ric, "I have never seen such commitment and dedication to a project. Most certainly, never in the industry. Everything moved so fast, and they weren't even construction people!"

That rich experience, coupled with God's unmistakable call, convinced both Ric and Carol to be open to whatever God would have for them. (Amazingly, when Ric returned home from Tucson, Carol was in accord with his new vision of ministry.)

The "whatever" turned out to be supervising over two hundred seventy-five volunteers on the 2.4 million-dollar construction project in Huntington Beach, and fifty apartments at the International Linguistic Center (ILC) in Dallas. (More about these projects in later chapters.)

In addition to his work as Senior Construction Superintendent at the ILC construction project, Ric is also responsible for the training of most of the new WA construction supervisors going to the field. In some cases, this is a two-year training program in which supervisors are trained in all facets of construction, including concrete work, insulation, framing, roofing, drywalling, finishing and more.

While these skills are indeed vital, the supervisor must be, in Ric's words, "A people person. We can't have supervisors coming unglued every time a volunteer drops his new level!"

"So much of our work involves ministering to the volunteers—affirming, building up, encouraging. Because we don't know about their backgrounds or life circumstances, we need mature, spiritually-sensitive supervisors who know how to make the people under them the most successful and fulfilled they can be."

The crucial ingredients for "The Tucson Project" were people: The Sengs, plus John Crain, Ernie Comte and others from the WA Tucson Chapter and the WA Construction Ministry team. They were challenged to meet the need of fifty translators from Mexico who were suddenly denied visa extensions and overnight were without homes and a permanent work place to continue their Bible translation ministry. In a step of audacious faith, the Tucson Chapter said, "We will trust, we will risk, because we believe God would have us accept this challenge." Working hand-in-glove with the Tucson Chapter, the WA board placed "The Tucson Project" on the 1981 fall banquet series to alert other construction volunteers to this unique opportunity for service in the U.S. and to raise the required twenty-five thousand dollars "seed money." The Lord answered both objectives, and when construction began, that twenty-five thousand dollars was multiplied to seventy-five thousand. "Such is the experience," said a godly sage, "of those who live their lives bold under God."

Several other construction projects were under way

in the early eighties. To help the WA constituency understand their scope, the *Newsletter* published two short articles. One, written by John Bender and titled, "Come Build With Us," gave a quick overview of the developing construction ministry:

> Since WA's first small construction project in 1968 for Wycliffe's North America Branch in Alaska (eighteen thousand four hundred dollars), our construction efforts have been geared to helping Wycliffe take the gospel "where Christ was not known" (Romans 15:20).
>
> During these fourteen years, hundreds of construction volunteers have traveled thousands of miles to give translators homes, clinics, airstrips, classrooms, libraries, translation space, utilities, telephone systems, and housing for language helpers.
>
> Last year three hundred twenty-two volunteers worked in ten countries, completing eighteen projects. So eager were the translators to use their new facilities that a couple of times they practically pushed us off the job. Construction value to Wycliffe totaled five hundred fifty-seven thousand dollars. Praise God!
>
> This year plans call for work in Kenya, Togo, Peru, Chile, Indonesia, and the United States. These plans include staff/student housing at Wycliffe's training center in Dallas, Texas, two new translation centers in Africa, a translation center in the remote Bird's Head region of Indonesia, and other projects.
>
> Many ingredients go into doing a professional job, not the least of which are good supervisors and superintendents. Along with full-time

supervisors Wes Syversen and Lonnie Waldner, we have the expertise of part-time supervisor Elroy Condit, and in training are Rich Hilton and John Ellis. In addition to recruiting construction volunteers, we're always on the lookout for capable supervisors.

WA is developing a new program called "Man Alive" (which originated in a California church) for interested congregations and mission-oriented people. This allows groups of individuals in local areas to directly participate in mission work on Wycliffe fields and share their experience in regular church fellowship. These active lay missionaries are providing a new dimension to churches' mission programs.

Volunteers tell me this experience is changing their lives... that they'll never be the same again. Seeing Wycliffe translators giving hidden people God's Word in their languages and then teaching them to read it makes a deep impression. Building takes on an importance never felt before because they know from firsthand experience they're helping in Bible translation.

As Wycliffe begins work in new languages, we'll need more construction crews to build training centers, housing, and translation facilities and to install utilities and telephones.

Come build with us!

John's second article, while short and to the point, showed the grand sweep of WA's geographical involvement and diversity. It also showed WA's faithfulness to Paul's scriptural injunction that each of us must not only work, but produce what is good. Under the tongue-twisting byline "Peru-Papuan Push Projects Well

Under Way," the report began:

> WA volunteers finished the Huanuco Trans-
> lation Center in the Andes Highlands in early
> February. Banquet funds of fifty thousand
> dollars were sent to purchase materials for this
> project, which is providing some great momen-
> tum to the translators in Peru.
>
> In Papua New Guinea, Wycliffe is using six
> thousand seven hundred dollars in banquet
> funds to purchase a four-wheel Toyota pickup
> for transportation to the remote Madang area.
> And a five thousand-dollar Ryan Stormscope
> will be purchased and installed in the Cessna
> 402. This aircraft equipment is a great safety
> feature, detecting and mapping thunderstorms
> while the plane is both on the ground and in the
> air. Substantial funds will also be provided as
> they come in later this year for a computer and
> language-helper housing in Papua New Guinea.
>
> Construction is now under way on the com-
> puter facility for the Australian Aborigines
> Branch in Darwin, Australia. A WA construction
> team of ten volunteers left in February. We're
> advancing thirty thousand dollars in banquet
> funds for this project.
>
> We praise God for early momentum on these
> exciting projects.

From his first days in Guatemala, Wycliffe's founder
William Cameron Townsend understood how much a
skilled layman could encourage missionary morale
and efficiency. No stranger to a hammer, saw and
chisel, he resolutely tackled repair jobs and add-ons
around his Guatemalan cornstalk house. Clearly, how-

ever, he was no carpenter. Part of a letter written from San Antonio, Guatemala on March 1, 1920, captures a young man's yearning for an organization not to be born for another forty-eight years:

> We moved over last Thursday. The house isn't complete as yet as the lamina or corrugated iron hasn't arrived. With the same corrugated iron we are going to make a little stable. Today I made a trip to Antigua and bought a saw, chisel, and monkey wrench so that we are getting pretty well stocked up on tools. If we make many more moves, I'll get to be a carpenter. I sure have wished for Lee [a carpenter] a good many times. As soon as possible, I have to make four windows. The glass is bought already . . . .

When WA did become a reality, much of its vision, entrepreneurial spirit and servant attitude came from Uncle Cam's modeling. Cam was a dreamer, but he knew more than most how to make his dreams come alive. He also knew how to motivate people. One gift (among many) was in making people feel wanted, needed and important. Over the years he received many honors, not only for personal selflessness, but also for the positive contribution WBT and SIL were making toward world peace. (Dr. Kenneth L. Pike, SIL Director Emeritus, has been nominated six times for the Nobel Peace Prize.) To recognize his unfailing commitment to Christian love, his practical, spiritual and humanitarian service to the world's ethnic minorities, Uncle Cam was decorated on October 28, 1981, by the then President of Peru, Fernando Belaunde, with the gold metal, "Order of the Sun," Peru's highest honor accorded a civilian foreigner.

Recognition by one's peers, however, cannot be compared to recognition by God. On April 23, 1982, William Cameron Townsend was ushered into the presence of his Lord to receive the highest of all honors, "Well done, good and faithful servant." His wife Elaine shared her personal thoughts and memories of Cam's last days in an open letter to all her many friends.

Dear Partners,
   My beloved Cam is now with the Lord whom he loved and served so faithfully. His promotion took place at 6 p.m. Friday, April 23, at the hospital in nearby Lancaster, South Carolina. Just two weeks previously we celebrated our thirty-sixth wedding anniversary, recalling so many precious ways the Lord has led us.
   On January 25, Cam was first taken to the hospital and Dr. Duke told us then he didn't have long to live as he had acute leukemia. Many of you prayed and the Lord gave him three months—some of the best we have known. All four children were able to spend time with Cam, even nine-day-old grandson Daniel Cameron Garippa whom Cam dedicated to the Lord along with Heather and Holly Tuggy.
   The last month we spent on Anna Maria Island in Florida at the lovely home of our dear friends Anthony and Sanna Rossi. Over fifty friends came to visit and each one went away encouraged by Cam's radiant smile and confidence in his Lord. Many times a day he would say, "God is SO good to me!" He told Anthony he had one foot in heaven. How good he felt when the doctor told him he would soon be there. Despite his illness, he hoped that one

more trip to the USSR would still be possible.

After that wonderful month in Florida, Cam was eager to get home again. We were home only one night when it was necessary to go to the hospital. Friends came from far and near and shared the blessing his life had been, as well as some of their goals for the future. Cam's brother Paul came from Oklahoma. How they did enjoy each other!

Many of you know that I love to be at every meeting here at our JAARS Center. However, the Lord did something very special for me those last three months, enabling me to much prefer to stay home at the side of my beloved, reading the Word and prayer letters and also praying and sharing some of his thoughts for the future. Everyone who was with him during his illness commented on what a sweet, loving man he was and to that I say a hearty AMEN!

The Lord provided for me by sending Jeanette Henny from Indiana to help with the household chores so I could devote my time to Cam. Another blessing was having our daughter Joy and her husband David Tuggy and five precious grandchildren staying in the apartment downstairs. How Cam loved to have the children in the home!

Cal Hibbard, Cam's faithful secretary for thirty-one years, worked many long hours taking care of urgent matters and tenderly giving Cam an hour-long massage each evening. What a team those two were! When the Lord called Cam home, it was Cal who handled all of the details for us. I wish you could have been here to see and feel the love shown at the memorial service. We had prayed that the timing would be just right. Only the Lord could have made it possible for our board members to be here, plus so many others.

Cam's body was laid to rest here at our Wycliffe/JAARS Center between the Mexico-Cardenas Museum and the new Alphabet Museum, both of which were inspired by Cam. After the graveside service, the WBT family gathered to share what Uncle Cam had meant in our lives. The meeting lasted three hours and no one wanted to leave. Many, many telegrams and written messages are coming from presidents, ambassadors, officials of many countries, friends and, of course, from our beloved co-workers. My thanks to each of you.

We are all hurting over the loss of our dear friend and leader. At the same time we sense, in a new way, the urgency of getting God's Word to the last tribe. May the Lord use Cam's death, even as He used his life, to hasten that blessed day! I am experiencing in a new way that the eternal God is MY refuge and underneath are the everlasting arms. Thank you for upholding me and the family.

                                        Elaine

Uncle Cam was dead, but most assuredly not his memory and what he taught about faith, prayer, vision, patient listening and love. Often this was a practical, simple kind of love, an almost insignificant gesture—a gift of cold lemonade offered to the man who collected his garbage on a hot day; a phone call just to say hello.

He knew that by reaching out in Christ's name with hospitality, in Christ's name, he was, in fact, extending him God's grace. Paul Tournier said, "Grace is more precious than medicine or advice." A person touched by the grace of God through one of his children, often receives spiritual healing and enrichment.

From the beginning, WA wanted to offer this grace to the WBT family. For this reason, hundreds of Associates have volunteered to participate in the Hospitality Roster. By 1982, more than two thousand Associates were listed on a newly revised and computerized hospitality list.

Over the years, the WA office in Orange has received hundreds of thank-you letters from WBT missionaries expressing their gratitude for this practical service. Scores of letters have also been received from hosting associates expressing the enrichment they received as a direct result of the visiting WBT workers. The following are examples of just a few:

> First year we had five guests. Second year, one guest. We want a lot more!—Peggy Comstock

> Our family really looks forward to the visits of the Wycliffe people. We have had wonderful fellowship.—Edith Flickner

> My wife and I have found this to be a delightful and rewarding experience. We originally entered this program expecting the traveling missionaries to bring the world to our doorstep, while we offered nothing more than a bedroom.—Russ and Karen Hoppe

> One young couple did not plan to use our home, but their car broke down outside our home. They spent the night and we helped them catch a flight back to Dallas. He and a friend

drove back and towed the car to Dallas and still
made it in time to attend the SIL training in
Norman, Oklahoma. We have become good
friends with the Ralph Ricco family. We love
them and are glad they feel at ease with us in our
home.—Al Walvoord

Praise God! What a blessing it is to have the
Wycliffe people in our home to share what God
is doing in the world. Thank you for this special
joy.—Virginia L. Schilliger

Last summer Wycliffe visitors were having
car trouble. While they were visiting us, we
introduced them to a mechanic friend. The
mechanic and his family are now in training as
WBT career supporters. Every WBT visitor has
been a blessing. Send more!—Gene and Sophia
Haas

My home has been dedicated to serve his
servants. It may be used as a place to get away
for a rest, relaxation and rejuvenation.—Juanita
Fike

It's so neat welcoming God's people and
having instant fellowship in Him!—Clyde and
Mary Lou Fisher

Occasionally the WA office receives a letter requesting
that their name be taken off the mailing list. Sometimes
no exact reason is given and the office wonders why.
But some letters from Associates with such requests
have been accepted with delight:

Note, as of August, please take our name off the Hospitality Roster. The Lord sent the exact WBT missionary to our home to encourage us in our plans at just the right time. Praise God, we will be joining WBT in August!—Dennis and Mary Meulemans

It was at a Wycliffe Associates banquet in 1977 that I decided to step out on faith and do what I had been thinking about for some time. That is, send off an application to SIL. One thing led to another and I found myself enjoying linguistic study and becoming more and more fond of Wycliffe and their purposes. It was during this time a friend pointed out that most careers have little eternal value, but a career in Wycliffe doing Bible translation would have much eternal value, because Jesus said, "My words will never pass away." These words have kept my pursuit of work with Wycliffe in focus.

In the interim, God has blessed me with a wonderful wife. And she also is convinced of the importance of Bible translation. Together we have begun a program of study at SIL. We have been assigned to the North America Branch.—Bill and Norma Jean Jancewicz

One WA distinctive is its team spirit that responds to need when asked. This letter exemplifies this element between a translator and Associate.

July 31, 1982

Dear Wycliffe Associates,
We'd like to thank you for your efforts to provide hospitality for those of us serving with

Wycliffe, and thought you might be interested
in one of our recent contacts with a family on
the Hospitality Roster.

When we returned from Ecuador in May, we
were traveling with our daughter, Penny (also of
the Ecuador Branch) and granddaughter. Their
home church is in Nashville, Tennessee, so we
were looking at the roster for a place for the rest
of us to stay a few days while Penny visited her
church and friends. We found *one* name for the
Nashville suburb of Franklin where Penny was
to stay with friends.

We called the people on the roster the day
before we left Atlanta, but were apologetically
told they couldn't take us because the lady of the
household had had major surgery, been in the
hospital two weeks, and would be returning
home the day we were to arrive in town. "But,"
continued the gentleman, "call back in two
hours and we'll tell you where you *can* stay."
Wasn't that a nice gesture?

Two hours later we called back and were told,
"We've been discussing the situation and have
decided that God is trying to tell us something.
We've been on the hospitality list for about two
years and nobody has ever called us before. We
want you to come and to stay with us. Maybe
you can be a help to us!"

Normally we wouldn't even consider going to
stay with someone fresh out of the hospital,
especially people we'd never even met, but in
view of their comments and recognizing that
God does indeed work in wondrous and myste-
rious ways, we accepted the invitation.

What a blessing that visit was to us (and,

hopefully, to their family). It was fun to get acquainted with them, to share the things of the Lord in spiritual fellowship and to help around the house and yard a bit as we enjoyed their hospitality. But one of the special blessings of that stay was seeing the delightful bond of friendship between their fourteen-year-old son and our fifteen-year-old son. Seldom have we seen two boys so much alike, and watching them enjoy one another was really special to both families.

So thanks again for your ministry. May God continue to bless you all.

In His love,
Gene, Virginia & Steven Smith

Chapter Nine

What a Difference a Team Makes

The body does not consist of one part but of many (1 Corinthians 12:14, Barclay).

There they were, five men as diverse as any five men could be—a real estate broker, a biochemist, a retired truck driver, a retired rancher and an associate pastor. But all worked in a natural rhythm with each other, united in vision, joyful in purpose and rich in fellowship. All this while sweating under a hot, tropical sun as they nailed roofing materials to the SIL guest house in Maluku, Indonesia. This was the early months of 1986, but the story of how these five men came to be in Indonesia, particularly in Maluku (formerly the Spice Islands) began three years earlier.

In 1971, when SIL signed its first agreement with the University of Cenderawasih in Irian Jaya, the branch faced enormous logistical and communication problems. Comprised of more than thirteen thousand islands, Indonesia, the fifth most populous country in the world, is also the world's largest archipelago. It straddles the equator from Asia to Australia in a huge three thousand-mile crescent.

With just over two hundred SIL members, the Indonesia Branch has worked with limited funds and personnel to fulfill its contractual agreements with the Ministry of Education to study the twenty-six languages in Irian Jaya. There are also seven language groups each in Sulawesi and Maluku.

Until 1982, the branch focused mainly on languages in Irian Jaya and Sulawesi. Then SIL member Chuck Grimes, son of Dr. Joseph and Barbara Grimes from the Mexico Branch, received an invitation from Mission Aviation Fellowship. They wanted a survey of Northern Maluku and asked Chuck to assist them.

When Chuck returned from Maluku, he enthusiastically believed God would have SIL begin a work there as well. For all the right reasons—lack of personnel and finances, and the enormous work load facing the branch as it fulfilled its contractual agreements in Irian Jaya and Sulawesi—the administration felt it would be better to wait a few years. But Chuck, along with Bob Critchfield, then chairman of the SIL Executive Committee, and Dick Hugoniot, then director of SIL's work in Indonesia, began to believe perhaps God would have the branch take a step of faith and look for ways to work with Maluku's ethnic peoples.

In February 1983, Dick Hugoniot and Bob Critchfield did a further survey of Maluku, and as they studied the Scriptures together, the Lord encouraged them from Deuteronomy not to be discouraged, but to go and take possession of the land.

Later, they spoke with the vice-rector of the University of Pattimura (under whom SIL would work in Maluku), who said, "When I was in England, I ran across a school at Horsleys Green. I was impressed with what they were doing. From what you have told me, it sounds as if your SIL program is very much like theirs."

Hardly believing his ears, Bob said, "Do you know, sir, it's the same organization?"

Encouraged by the vice-rector's favorable reception, and later by Dick and Bob's report, the Indonesia Executive Committee voted to begin work in Maluku. Chuck and his wife Barbara, Howard and Dee Sheldon and Bob and Joan Critchfield were the first three couples assigned there. Bob was appointed director.

It's all very well, of course, to agree to begin a new work. But then comes the hard work—finding personnel and finances. After Bob, on behalf of SIL, signed the contract with the University of Pattimura, he met with Chuck Grimes and invited him to "dream a bit" about facilities and costs.

"Let's look down the road five years," said Bob. "Let's ask ourselves what kind of equipment and facilities we'll need." (The university had given them land on which to build.) After several hours, Bob and Chuck estimated a figure of one hundred sixty-eight thousand dollars. Shortly after this session with Chuck, Bob flew to Dallas for SIL and WBT's biennial conference. He and Dick Hugoniot met with Al Ginty and John Bender about how WA might help.

Enthused and filled with wonder about SIL developments in Maluku, Bob and Dick shared their vision with Al and John who, in turn, became enthusiastic. The practical aspects, however, did not escape them. Al asked if Bob had thought through what they needed and if they had a plan.

With a knowing smile, Bob said, "Glad you asked," and presented Al with a five-year plan for the Maluku Islands.

Al and John gave thoughtful consideration to Bob Critchfield's impressive plan. Said Al, "I don't think WA can handle the entire package, but perhaps if you could break your needs down into at least three units or phases, then we could handle this, providing we can get permission from the WBT administration. As you know, there are always more needs than we can handle and others are on the list ahead of you. But let's pray and trust God to see what He will do for you, and for us, too."

Much had to happen after the biennial conference, but in time the WBT administration approved Bob's plans and the young branch's special needs. Al agreed to proceed with a letter to the WA membership asking for fifty thousand dollars to begin the three-phase Operation Maluku. Phase One financed a linguistic survey to determine the Maluku translation needs. Phase Two included a vehicle and some basic equipment needs (chairs, typewriters, etc.) and an administration building. Phase Three was a guest house. (As of this writing, a hangar is also being constructed for the first JAARS Maluku plane.) Eager to see this young branch proceed, WA'ers responded enthusiastically to each need.

In 1983, when Bob asked JAARS for a plane to service their translators, JAARS said, "You might get on the list in about 1987."

"Impossible," said Bob, "we need a plane now."

"Well," said JAARS, "just put in your request and pray."

Amazingly, within six months after Bob's request, through a matching gift from WA, Maluku did in fact get a plane!

In 1985, during Phase Three, Bruce Miller who heads up WA's Missions Alive Ministry (an active part of John Bender's construction ministry), was planning a trip to Chicago. One day he received a phone call from Ben Cross, the pastor of the Dry Creek Bible Church in

Montana. The pastor said neither he nor his church knew much about Wycliffe Associates, but that they would like to know more. Always eager to explain the Missions Alive ministry, Bruce said, "The ministry is designed to benefit the local church. We have found that when a congregation becomes enthused about missions and sends a team of men and women to a field, or becomes involved in some other practical way, most often they receive as much or more blessing than the person or persons who receive their practical help."

"That's wonderful," said the pastor. "I wonder if you could be our Sunday morning speaker during our missions conference in October."

"Yes," said Bruce. "I'll be in Chicago during that week and will be able to work in a flight to Montana on my return to California."

Circumstances, however, caused the cancellation of the Chicago trip and Bruce was left with the one commitment in Dry Creek. As he thought about his heavy schedule and the expenses involved traveling to what he thought was a tiny country church, he almost canceled his commitment. "But," said Bruce, "I just didn't have the liberty of the Spirit to pick up the phone and tell them I wasn't coming."

When Bruce arrived at the Dry Creek Bible Church, he found it to be exactly as he had imagined—a white clapboard building with a traditional bell spire and a Bible verse painted over the door. But the stereotype ended there. He found a vibrant mix of two hundred fifty young, middle-aged and older people excited about their faith, their church and their neighbors— near and far.

Bruce didn't remember everything he said during those two Sunday morning services. He did, however, tell the congregation about the Indonesian service

opportunities, a natural since WA was then involved in
Maluku. The pastor had also mentioned that some
people were particularly interested in that country.

Warmed by the congregation's unexpected enthusiasm
for the Missions Alive Ministry, Bruce returned to
Southern California happy that he had fulfilled his
commitment. And that was that. As with other such
meetings, he simply left the challenge with them.

Responses to WA Missions Alive presentations most
often take several months or more to formulate. Dry
Creek Bible Church, however, responded within weeks.
Not until May 1986, though, did Bruce and other WA
staff fully appreciate or understand what God had done
to bring five of these men to Indonesia, and what it had
meant to the entire Dry Creek congregation. Pastor
Cross sent Bruce the following letter to explain:

> Dry Creek, Montana
> May 20, 1986

> Subject: MISSIONS ALIVE IN MONTANA
> Our "Missionaries" to Indonesia

> Dear Bruce:
> In the beginning, it was only a dream; one of
> those "wouldn't-it-be-great-if" kind of things
> that I shared with a group of men in a disciple-
> ship class. But in the back of my mind, I knew it
> was unrealistic to think that anyone from our
> little country church in Montana would seriously
> consider leaving his family and job for six
> weeks to work with Wycliffe Associates in the
> Maluku Islands of Indonesia. The economy in
> our area was too low, the cost too high and the
> location of the project too far out of the way for
> us to participate.

However, a few weeks later a real estate broker in our church approached me after a Sunday morning service. He said he had been thinking and praying about the need in Indonesia and believed that God wanted him to go. It wasn't a week later that another member of the church, a biochemist, said that he would give up his job, if necessary, to serve God for six weeks on the mission field.

I think it was about then I realized that the Lord was stirring something up that barriers like a poor economy in Montana and the expanse of the Pacific Ocean simply couldn't stop. Before long, three other men—a retired rancher, a retired truck driver, and even the associate pastor—said they would go.

Could it be possible God was calling five men from the Body at Dry Creek, Montana, to go overseas at a cost of twelve thousand five hundred dollars and we had only three months to raise the money and go through all the necessary steps of preparation for passports, visas, etc.? A few people in the congregation even quietly grumbled about the whole idea. They questioned the motives of the men, surmising that they were going on some kind of vacation adventure, and besides, how could we possibly raise that kind of money in this little church?

But again, our God is bigger than any problem that stood in the way, and the vast majority of the people, who were well-informed, knew better than to feel that way about the project. We proceeded prayerfully with the plans, and a few weeks later, at a Saturday evening "kick-off" dinner, the church gave nine thousand five hundred dollars! A rush of excitement filled the congregation that Sunday when we announced the results. The complaining quit. It was obvious to all that the Lord's blessing was on this ministry. At the end of three months, the church had raised twelve thousand seven hundred dollars! We surpassed what originally seemed an impossible amount!

There are so many wonderful lessons we have learned through this experience that I know will have a lasting impact on our church. Few things have brought our people together more powerfully than their mutual participation in this project. Missions is no longer a detached and distant thing to them. We all sensed the sacrifice, the risk, and the joy of "getting involved" in world evangelism in this more personal dimension. Sure, we support several missionaries on the foreign field, but to many of the people they're just pictures on the wall or spots on a map. Now a part of our own local church was going. Suddenly missions seemed more relevant, more real.

Without a doubt the children were greatly influenced by the sending of these men. On a weekly basis, one of the five "missionaries" would visit the children's Sunday School opening time to share their excitement, but also their personal fears and needs, as they prepared to go. "Missionary Andy" was afraid of flying. "Missionary Gregg" might lose his job. Before leaving, "Missionary Tom" had many major business transactions that had to be completed, and the list went on. It was so thrilling to hear our children pray for these men at night, around the supper table and in Sunday School. Missions was no longer something strange to them. People they knew and loved were leaving home to serve God in another part of the world.

The children were also challenged to be involved in giving money to the project. We set a goal of seventy-five dollars for them to reach with only one rule. They couldn't simply ask Mom and Dad for the money. They were to work, doing special chores, etc., and then give from their earnings as the Lord led them. They raised over one hundred dollars. To say the least, they were excited!

In so many beautiful ways, the Lord has taught us and changed us in the sending of these men, but the greatest growth was apparent in the "missionaries" when they returned. With their firsthand experience on the field, they were no longer limited to missions theory. Now they had missions practice, and their ministry in Indonesia was only a start. They are presently reshaping our attitudes and vision for missions. They know what it means to face culture shock, to receive a letter from home, and most of all, to see the vast spiritual wasteland that is yet unreached for Christ in this world. One of the men is making plans to return to Indonesia for three months with his wife this fall.

The Dry Creek Bible Church will never be the same because of what God did in our lives and the lives of five very special men in the winter months of 1986 with Wycliffe Associates.

Sincerely in the Lord,
Pastor Ben Cross

While WA has uniquely linked the lay Christian to mission outreach, it has always supported the importance of involving the church in world mission. The Dry Creek Bible Church is a wonderful example of this. The WA files are replete with testimonials from congregations across the United States, Canada and elsewhere who have been enriched by their participation in the Missions Alive program.

One recent example began with yet another telephone call to Bruce Miller. This time the call came from Steve Goold, pastor of Emmanuel Evangelical Free Church in Burbank, California. When Bruce received Pastor Goold's call, he could hardly believe his ears. Said Pastor Goold, "We have a twenty-man crew set to go on a missions trip to Africa, but the project didn't materialize. Now we have twenty men who are anxious to do something positive on the mission field. We have funding from the church and we have the time. The only thing lacking is a meaningful project. Do you have a spot where we as a church-sponsored team might serve a specific need?"

Two weeks before, Helen Neuenswander (a nurse) and Mary Shaw, a translator team working among Guatemala's Achi people, had asked WA to help build four "patient care units." They would be an addition to the hospital established through Helen's clinic work in Cubulco.

Bruce explained to Pastor Goold that many volunteers from all across the country were working on this project. A group of twenty men might not be necessary —"except," said Bruce, "we do have two open weeks in June."

"God's timing is always perfect," said Pastor Goold, "because it just so happens that those are the exact dates when our men would be free to go."

Pastor Goold and the team from Emmanuel immediately began to pray and make plans for their trip to Guatemala. Emmanuel's missions committee, who had helped select the men, continued their involvement by praying for each team member. The committee also brought the men before the church in a special time of sharing and prayer for the project.

Meanwhile, one team member, Gary Baker, a cinematographer, called Bruce and shared his desire to produce a film showing the men interacting with the Achi people as they worked in partnership on the hospital construction.

"This could be a joint venture between Emmanuel and WA," said Gary. "It could be used to show how a partnership between the church and WA serves to enrich not only a people in a developing country, but the local congregation who themselves have taken a step of faith to serve in a mission outreach."

To allay Bruce's fears that this might be an amateurish production, Gary explained his credentials and list of film credits including work done for Billy Graham through World Wide Pictures and Moody Bible Institute. The outcome was a splendid production † that goes far beyond merely documenting movements, gestures and work done. Rather, the film captures the viewer's heart and mind by revealing the nature of people working and fellowshipping together with a common purpose and love for God. The men themselves tell honestly and without artifice what living and working in a Guatemalan mountain village for two weeks has meant to

---

† The film, entitled *From Brick and Mortar,* is available through the WA office in Orange, California, and is suitable for showing to Sunday School classes, to Christian Education groups and others interested in knowing how WA's Missions Alive Ministry can serve their church.

their own spiritual growth.

By the mid-eighties, John Bender and Wes Syverson had construction crews and superintendents not only in Guatemala and Indonesia, but in Suriname, Papua New Guinea, Peru, the Solomon Islands, Chile, England, Texas and California. (WA's own offices were long-overdue for expansion. In a kind of lend-lease, Jim Dykstra, with his wife Hendrine, came from Edmonton, Alberta, Canada, to oversee the WA expansion project.)

Wycliffe's British center at Horsleys Green, a former barracks for a boys' summer camp thirty miles west of London, was in desperate need of major renovations. This included new sewers, copper pipe, new kitchenettes and larger sleeping quarters and offices. This work and more was directed by WA Project Superintendent Chet Niles. Twenty-nine volunteers paid their own way to work for three weeks during some of England's worst spring weather—thirty-eight consecutive days of rain!

One couple, Jim and Vernena Crump, however, managed only a ten-day commitment. "At first," said Jim, "we wondered why the Lord wanted us to invest this much money for such a long trip for only ten days. But soon after our arrival, we had our answer. Ron Virrels, a support worker from Papua New Guinea, passed through the center and told us he was in charge of maintaining about one thousand typewriters, fifty of which were extremely difficult to repair. Little did he know I was a repair technician for the very company that manufactures those typewriters. I thought the Lord had brought me to England to work on the renovation project at Horsleys Green. As it turned out, the Lord allowed our paths to cross for a full day in order that I could share my technical knowledge and practical experience with this Wycliffe worker from Papua New Guinea."

Sometimes there are those who feel if they are not "hands," they are excluded from WA's hands-on ministry opportunities. One faithful reader of the *Newsletter*, Hero Bratt, felt a little like this as he read how Paul Doolittle, a mechanic from Santa Ana, California, volunteered his time to go to a field and repair automobiles for Wycliffe workers.

How unfortunate, thought Hero, that I don't have a talent like this to offer Wycliffe Associates. As he was lamenting his lack of mechanical skill, he turned the page of the *Newsletter* and noticed a long list of books needed by Wycliffe personnel. Ah, thought Hero, now here is something I can do. Since he was vice president of a large publishing company, he made available, at a substantial discount, a whole series of reference books. Later he established an agreement with WA to give Wycliffe personnel dealer discounts on all upcoming and back-listed books. Clearly, this exemplifies how one member of the Body creatively shared his resources with others for their mutual benefit.

David Ludwick, a journeyman electrician from New Hampshire, and his employer, David Street, owner of Street Electric provide another example of shared resources. As of this writing, Dave Ludwick is involved in Lancaster, Pennsylvania's Willow Valley Apartment Project, which will help provide affordable housing for Wycliffe missionaries at WBT's northeast regional office.

Most WA construction volunteers come from the U.S. and Canada. Some include Gordon Dykstra, along with his wife Joan and their two children, from Edmonton, Alberta. (Gordon is the son of Jim Dykstra who oversaw WA's office renovation in Orange, California.) And from Southern California in May 1987 came Wayne and Lois West.

One day, while he was working with Dave Ludwick, Wayne asked him how he came to work for WA.

"It's an amazing provision from God," said Dave. "About a year ago I went to Haiti on a church-sponsored construction project. When I returned from what, for me, was a life-changing experience, I began to feel that working in construction-related ministries would be a great way to serve the Lord. About that time I read about WA's construction ministries in their *Newsletter* and had that same feeling come over me that I should consider this as a full-time option for service. But how could I? I had a house payment and a wife and two children to support. I decided I would just pray about my feelings and leave it with the Lord.

"Then one day out of the blue my boss said, 'You know, Dave, the Lord has been speaking to me. He has laid it upon my heart to do something for Wycliffe. But it hasn't been clear to me what exactly I should do—give money, or what? The thought did come to me that it might be a good idea if I helped you go with Wycliffe. If you feel this is something God would have you do, I will pay your wages and benefits and I'd like to furnish you with a van.'"

How right Paul was to use the metaphor of the human body to describe the Church. This Body with its many parts, each unique, functions in its assigned sphere of service and usefulness for the common good and blessing of the whole, the Church of Jesus Christ.

Chapter Ten

Maturity Based on Prayer

J esus' ministry was characterized by audaciousness. He refused to be bound by tradition or the status quo. And throughout the centuries, the Christian community has tried in different and creative ways, to give form and meaning to his modeling and the Great Commission. In a way, that's what WA is all about. More particularly, it's about people who have been motivated by love and a desire to support and be active participants in what God is doing through Wycliffe Bible Translators.

This book is also an attempt to recount the emergence of an organization into the community of world mission. An organization that in twenty years has grown far beyond the dreams and intentions of its three energetic and nonconformist founders: Dale Kietzman, Bill Butler and Rudy Renfer.

"The early eighties," said one observer, "was a time of learning for WA. It was a time to gain independence, just like all adolescents must do. But now WA is twenty years old and moving into maturity. This maturity is reflected in the improved quality of their programs. They have continued to train all area directors and banquet speakers. Speakers are trained to boil down all they have to say into a strong, powerful thirty-minute presentation—not to be slick, but to be effective."

One of their astonishing statistics is that as many as sixty percent of those coming to the banquets are hearing about Wycliffe for the first time. WA realizes the importance of professionalism and integrity as they present the challenge and opportunity for involvement in WA's many service opportunities.

Another indication of growth from adolescence to adulthood has been the increasing global scope of their service. In 1987, WA volunteers served in Colombia, Indonesia, England, the Philippines, Ghana, Canada, Australia, Senegal; Lancaster, Pennsylvania; Dallas, Texas; and Huntington Beach, California. The voluminous details created by these simultaneous projects are coordinated by Beckie Roberts, assistant to the Director of Missions Alive. Beckie communicates with hundreds of volunteers, matching their skills and availability with particular construction needs in ten to fifteen different countries. She arranges for visas, plane tickets and other travel-related items, plus maintaining computer records of more than two thousand volunteers at any one time.

Down through the centuries, the consciousness of Christ's living presence has drawn believers to prayer. As Paul Tournier said so beautifully, "The daily habit of placing oneself, resolutely before God (in prayer) activates a deep sense of reliance on God in virtue of which life can be lived courageously, joyously, creatively, and in gratitude.... Faith born out of prayer and meditation breeds not only the sense of adventure of living, but achieves a radical transformation of the attitudes, values and purposes."†

In 1984, when Al interviewed Deborah Smith for

---

† Quoted in *Personal Living, an Introduction to Paul Tournier* by Monroe Peaston, (Harper & Row, N.T., 1972), p.79.

WA, the Lord seemed to impress him to ask her about prayer. Deborah said she was interested in prayer and that, in her mind, nothing was more important or effective in furthering God's Kingdom. She proved a natural choice to initiate WA's new Prayer Watch program.

Said Deborah, "The first thing I did was to start a morning prayer time for each department Tuesday through Friday. Monday was already established as our collective devotional time. My conviction was that we would serve the Lord more effectively if we began the day together with the Lord and our fellow workers. This assumption has proven to exceed our expectations in unifying the staff and multiplying our effectiveness. I also felt we had to practice as a staff what we were calling our membership to do.

"My next step was to try to remedy what Al saw as a deficiency in the home office's regular communication with the WA board between board meetings. The full board meets thrice yearly and the executive committee three other times during the year. We send a packet of information to each board member before the six meetings occur, but little other significant communication is sent to them. I began to call eight board members every other week thereby reaching all twenty-four every six weeks. I asked about any prayer requests they might have, gave each a mini-report on WA and shared a few important prayer requests from WA's ministries. I then compiled a summary sheet that included the eight members' requests, along with the WA update and requests. Each board member and all the staff receive these sheets. They have helped us stay in touch with each other between board gatherings and served to help the board members feel more tied to the home office all year round.

"After getting our own house in order, we began to reach out to the WA membership. During the spring and summer of 1985, I began identifying the Wycliffe Associates who were especially committed to prayer for our ministry. I used the notes we frequently receive from members telling us of their prayers for us. Also in a couple of our special letters, we had asked people to let us know if they would pray the featured project through to completion. To each of these people I sent a personal letter thanking them for their prayers, updating them on the project for which they had been praying, announcing our new prayer ministry (which by now we had named Prayer Watch after Isaiah 62:6) and inviting them to become charter watchmen. Many responded affirmatively.

"Then in September we installed two telephone lines (WATS) we called "Watchlines." One for California, the other for the other forty-seven contiguous states. We notified all of our Prayer Watchmen of the toll-free Watchline phone number and the calls began to come in. My goal by the end of the year was to have one hundred Prayer Watchmen. We had more than three hundred! And the following year, the Lord also exceeded our goals as we grew to over one thousand."

People who visit Deborah in her office and hear the answering machines clicking on and rewinding often ask, "Doesn't that noise drive you crazy?" "Not at all!" says Deborah, "Each click means another person is praying for our ministry and that fires me up."

One of Deborah's favorite comments about the effectiveness of the prayer ministry, came from a woman in Texas who said, "You're not only helping us pray for the needs of Bible translation, but you're also helping us as Christians to organize our prayer life."

Another example of answered prayer comes from a

memo dated November 22, 1985, written by Mike Yoder
who now heads up the publications ministries.

> A couple of months ago we asked you to pray
> for Lonnie Waldner as he went to South America
> to set up several construction projects. He has
> returned from his trip and has now collected the
> supplies and equipment needed for these pro-
> jects and has packed them in a sea container. It
> weighs thirty-five thousand pounds and is due
> to arrive in Peru this week. We need to pray that
> it will get through customs by December 31 in
> order that the contents will be available to the
> crew when they arrive in January.

But despite this request, the construction materials
and equipment were still tied up in customs when the
crew of volunteers arrived. Then on February 22, the
Prayer Watchline gave this report:

> The huge container of equipment has finally
> been released for the Peru construction project.
> They have unloaded everything and are moving
> full steam ahead on that much-needed facility
> for our translators. We don't know why the Lord
> chose to delay the release of the equipment, but
> isn't is wonderful we can rest on Romans 8:28?

During the delay, the WA construction staff had no
other avenue open but prayer and faith—that God
would work this out for his good. Often we never know
exactly how God will work in a difficult situation. The
believer is called upon to rest in the sovereign will of God
and wait for eternity to reveal life's "whys." But in this
case, the "good" that came from this delay was revealed

in a matter of weeks. John Bender was so overwhelmed with the news that he recorded this message on the March 7, 1986, Watchline report:

> Hello! This is John Bender, Vice President for Construction Ministries speaking to you on the Wycliffe Associates Watchline. We received some exciting news this week, and it may explain part of the reason why the Lord delayed the release of the container in Peru. Dave and Marie Del Medico, our construction superintendents in Lima, had to go to the customs office repeatedly in an effort to gain the release of the container. In the process, they befriended Yvon, one of the customs officials. Dave and Marie took the opportunity to share the Lord with Yvon, and just last week she committed her life to Christ. Isn't that exciting? Now the Del Medicos are sharing Christ with Yvon's family, and they've asked us to pray for their salvation. We'll be sure to keep you posted. God truly does work all things together for good.

Those people, serious about prayer, know God sometimes answers immediately, as when Jesus stilled the storm for the disciples. On other occasions, God may delay the answer to produce fortitude, confidence and perseverance. Such a situation occurred in Quebec late one fall, and was reported by Wes Syverson, WA's Director of Utilities.

> Lack of water was slowing Bible translation for seven language groups in Quebec. It was so bad at the Roberval Center that translation workshops had to be cancelled.
> The teams there asked WA for help and after

their victorious well-drilling experiences in Peru, superintendent Dave Beaty, volunteers Jay and Pat Breazeale, and Jerry Jameson went to Canada to drill wells at Roberval.

But almost at once they ran into trouble. The bit stuck at two hundred thirty feet and then they had a blowout with water gushing onto the workers. The sub-zero temperature created a hazard and forced them to halt the project until spring.

Some professionals in the well-drilling business advised us to abandon the project and count our losses.... which added up to ten thousand dollars. We felt, however, that we should not treat lightly such valuable equipment. We enlisted the prayer support of our WA staff, the WA Board of Trustees, and our Associates on our prayer lists, asking for God's help.

When spring came, a crew returned to Roberval to complete the water wells and on the third day God answered our prayers. Not only did the bit come out, but the hole where it had lodged was large enough to serve as a well that provided seventeen gallons per minute, as much as the pump could handle!

Truly the nearly-impossible situation in Roberval turned into a great blessing—another example of how the Lord answers above and beyond our needs.

As the Prayer Watch program has matured, so has WA's relationship with WBT. In a June 1987 interoffice memo, President Al Ginty wrote: "Never in our twenty-year history has WA been closer and more in tune with all the underlying purposes of WBT. Never has there been closer family ties, unified ministry, and a sense of teamwork between our organizations. I can state with deep conviction that WA is simply meaningless without WBT. WA exists only to serve and help move forward in every practical way WBT's ministry of Bible translation. Therefore, our relationship is based on an assurance that everything WA does is done for WBT's benefit."

As Al reflected on WA's current progress and maturity, he gave credit to Bernie May, Director of WBT's U.S. Division, for his intuitive and visionary leadership. "His cooperation and encouraging leadership," said Al, "has resulted in huge blessings and major benefits both for WA and WBT during his six-year administration (1981-1987)."

And so WA's purposes and vision continue to grow and bear fruit as lay volunteers become directly involved in missions. Like installing the two-hundred-line telephone system recently in a translation center in Australia. It was donated by an Associate and then refurbished and assembled in Conway, Arkansas (one of seven WA warehouses around the country), by Associate David Reynolds and his crew of WA volunteers.

And from Eugene, Oregon, to Joplin, Missouri, from Lansing, Michigan, to Sarasota, Florida, and Youngstown, Ohio—all across the nation, once each spring and once again in the fall, seven WA area directors with their Wycliffe speakers fresh from the mission field fan out regularly to four hundred twenty cities, towns and communities (over an eighteen-month cycle) with the story of what God is doing through Bible translation. The logistics for planning these banquets require dedicated banquet reservation Associates who work with WA area directors and the Banquet Ministry Coordinator at headquarters.

Monies raised continue to provide equipment and

services for Wycliffe's worldwide Bible translation ministry. Equipment like computers for national translators in Cameroon, Indonesia, the Philippines and Papua New Guinea; much-needed vehicles in Ghana, West Africa and the Solomon Islands. For a copy machine for the Malaysia Branch; and for a room addition in Paramaribo, Suriname; for an emergency radio system in the Brazilian rain forest and a printing arts building in Dallas, Texas. And besides tangible equipment, WA banquet funds help launch language and linguistic surveys to predetermine where Scripture translation is needed. On and on it goes—more than forty-five thousand Associates, partners together, doing a job that could not be done without the participation of such a team.

The two ministries that have contributed most to WA's impact on Bible translation, and exemplify this team spirit are the banquet and construction ministries. Both have been sketched in earlier chapters. However, because of their significant contribution to Bible translation it seems appropriate to conclude this volume with two stories, one from each, that illustrate their effect on staff, volunteers and Wycliffe at large. First, the banquet ministry.

Twice each year, fall and spring, seven experienced Wycliffe missionaries (usually fresh from their field assignments and eager to tell their first-person stories), are teamed with seven equally experienced and energetic WA area directors (and their regional, lay banquet coordinators) for a six-week series of banquet meetings in seven areas around the country.

One reason for the enthusiasm area directors have for their work may have to do with the "stepping stones" the Spirit of God used to involve them in missions and ultimately, WA. For example, before joining WA in

1978 as WA's Southeast Area Director, Pete Brouillette, with his wife Shirley took a group of young people from their home Bible study to tour the SIL facility in Mexico City.

The official tour guide for the SIL center was Al Williams. (He and his wife Eunice would later become WA's North Central area director team.) Said Pete, "We thought if we gave these young people a frontline mission experience, they would be better able to assess whether or not God was leading them into missionary service. We never dreamed at the time we would ourselves be stirred to consider becoming part of the Wycliffe team."

Pete's use of the word "team" was most appropriate, because it was a team effort that helped them take that important leap of faith. Pete was encouraged by the Williams' input in Mexico, and by perennially enthusiastic Wycliffe booster and editor of *Beyond*, Bob Griffin, when he said, "God could use a guy like you in Wycliffe." Then long-time JAARS executive Bill Sasnett, encouraged and helped Pete fill out a preliminary questionnaire.

Other "team members" included Joe France who, after finding Pete's questionnaire on a desk, took time to make an important long-distance phone call. WA board member Billy Gibson and WA banquet speakers Marilyn Laszlo and Bev Entz also played a part, as did Uncle Cam, Ken Pike, Cal Hibbard, Jim Baptista, and Al Ginty. These people worked together as a team, sensitive to God's calling in their own lives and his potential calling in the lives of others.

Pete became Southeast Area Director in 1978, a year after filling out his preliminary questionnaire (not actually required for a WA area director). For the first two years he believed his job was to raise money for various mission projects. "John Bender and his construction crews were fanning out all over the world responding to needs requested by Wycliffe's international office in Dallas," said Pete. "I thought my job was to work as hard as I could to help provide those needed funds to get the job done on the mission field."

This was an understandable assumption. But the harder Pete worked, the less he seemed to accomplish. Interest in the banquets began to drop off and therefore faith promise monies from those banquets diminished.

But then two important experiences altered Pete's approach to his ministry. The first came from Al Ginty who, after reviewing Pete's work, said, "Are you ministering to lay people? Or are you using them to accomplish goals, to tally up numbers and bring in money?"

Said Pete, "Those words so shook me up, they drove me to my knees in prayer and to an in-depth search of the Scriptures."

Shortly after that encounter, Pete visited SIL's jungle translation center at Yarinococha, Peru. One evening while he was enjoying a particularly beautiful sunset out on the lake, God impressed Pete's mind with a new sense of direction. "It wasn't an audible voice," said Pete, "but clearly God was speaking to me and the message was, 'I want you to be the middle man.' "

Previously, Pete tried to be out front, pushing himself and his program to get the job done. Now the Lord was saying, "Pete, your job is to move among people and encourage them in love to become involved. The results are up to Me." When Pete returned home, one of the first questions he asked himself was, "What can I do for people; how can I minister to them?"

Intuitively, Pete realized that people respond best to friendship, built over time from common bonds and shared convictions. After praying for a hundred people

committed to pray for WA and the Southeast, Pete
began writing letters and making phone calls. His first
contacts included those who in the past had shown
some interest in WA—banquet coordinators, volunteers
on work parties and WA chapter leaders.

God took eighteen months to answer Pete's prayers,
but now he has a hundred people he calls his "Insiders."
"These," said Pete, "are people who are bound by
friendship and fellowship in the Gospel and are
committed to pray for WA's worldwide ministry on
behalf of Wycliffe Bible Translators."

The outgrowth of this new direction in Pete's ministry
has been a shift in area responsibilities. His workload,
reduced from a ten- to a four-state area, allowed him
more time to develop his primary ministry: building
relationships with WA'ers and working with WA
chapters. (There are fourteen WA chapters in two of his
states—North and South Carolina, more than any
other area.)

Emphasis on organizing committed prayer groups
and on building relationships which stress that *people*
are more important than their *money* has resulted in a
dramatic increase in banquet attendance and renewed
enthusiasm for WA projects. Said Pete, "We are, of
course, delighted with the way God is answering prayer
for the projects. How can we measure the effect on Bible
translation when a chapter raises money for a translator
in Africa to buy solar panels to operate her computer?
But in the midst of this increase, I realized we were
overlooking an important aspect of our ministry,
namely, recruitment of new translators and Wycliffe
workers."

Burdened by this oversight, Pete and Shirley, along
with the one hundred "Insiders" began to ask the Lord
for one serious mission candidate for each banquet.

"On an average, we conduct twenty-one banquets in twenty-eight days," said Pete, "and since we hold two banquet series a year, the Lord could raise up forty-two serious candidates each year. By 'serious candidate,' I mean someone who is willing to fill out the preliminary questionnaire and mail it in. I am happy to say that God has honored that prayer request at every single banquet!"

This same philosophy of building relationships also motivates the construction ministry. WA's Foreign Projects Coordinator Lonnie Waldner's personality may be the antithesis of Pete Brouillette's, but he also had to learn that work parties stimulated to spiritual growth produce eternal benefits that far exceed any construction work.

In 1979, fresh from college with a degree in welding and mechanical technology, Lonnie, at the invitation of Wes Syverson, "cut his eye teeth" on an airstrip Wes was building in Colombia. Three years later, Lonnie joined WA's Construction Ministries and went with twenty other men on a construction work party to Suriname. Said Lonnie, "I was impressed with the men God brought together for this project. One man from Canada became good friends with a seventy-eight-year-old man from Florida. For three weeks they worked side-by-side, the older man keeping right up with the younger for a full eight-hour day. They had wonderful fellowship together and when they left, it was as if each were saying good-bye to his very best friend."

For the next several years, Lonnie worked (often as superintendent) on projects in Indonesia, Peru, Colombia, Chile, Panama, Huntington Beach, California, and Waxhaw, North Carolina.

It was in 1981, however, while working on a translation building and duplex in Panama, that SIL's Panama

Director Bob Gunn, made the "difference" in Lonnie's life. "When I work, I never walk," said Lonnie. "I always run. For the first couple of years I pushed, pushed, pushed to get the jobs completed in the allotted time. I worked long hours every day except Sunday, and I expected others to do the same. One day, when I knew we had to do three weeks work in two, I took out my frustration on the director, Bob Gunn. In reality, I was pushing him to get me more help. I knew he was overtaxed, just like I was, but I pushed nonetheless.

"In the course of our conversation, Bob turned to me and said, 'You know, Lonnie, people are more important than the job.' At the time I strongly disagreed with him and said, 'Yes, but you don't understand. . . .' 'No,' said Bob, 'You don't understand. People really are more important.' I tried to justify my position and legitimize my reasons for pushing hard. But Bob just kept repeating that people were more important."

Several months later, when Lonnie began work on an important translation center in Peru, Bob Gunn's words came back to him. "It was during that project," said Lonnie, "that I began to understand that people have needs. When I took time to listen and people had an opportunity to express themselves, the work seemed to progress more effectively. This came home to me when one fellow on the project, newly separated from his wife, just needed a listening ear. He was deeply upset and I spent a lot of time with him. Some days, it seemed we didn't get much accomplished. Yet in spite of the time out, the job moved ahead on schedule."

Now not only sensitive to the volunteers' interpersonal needs, Lonnie has also developed a sensitivity to those who lack experience in handling local building materials. The principal construction material in Latin America is cement, from which they make concrete blocks for walls, reinforced concrete columns, concrete floors and poured concrete roofs. In 1982, as Lonnie wondered how to efficiently use the unskilled (in concrete construction) volunteer help for the Peruvian Huarez translation center, he noticed this country had large amounts of high-quality lumber available from mills in the jungle. Curiously, very little was being used for major construction. If Lonnie used the readily-available lumber for a stud-framing construction, he could make the job easier for his volunteers. (Most anyone can drive a nail!) On the other hand, if he decided on this route, he faced two major obstacles. One, how to make the buildings structurally strong enough to pass the earthquake code. And two, how to satisfy the architectural consultant's insistence that the buildings conform to the local design (all built from concrete block).

Taking his cue from the California building code which is also concerned about earthquakes, Lonnie decided to try something never before attempted in that part of Peru. Checking his engineering in the States, Lonnie used local lumber and constructed a conventional U.S. frame building. The earthquake code was passed by using shear paneling. To achieve the desired concrete-block look, the outside walls were roughly stuccoed.

Said Lonnie, "Some of the people were skeptical about how these buildings would look. But when they were completed and the stucco applied, no one could tell they hadn't been built from the usual concrete materials. We were also able to show the local people a less expensive way to construct their houses and buildings.

"To supervise a project to completion is very exciting for me," said Lonnie, "but I want to emphasize that the best part of being a WA superintendent is watching the volunteers grow in their spiritual life. The buildings we build are all important and necessary. One day, however, they will all be destroyed. But the spiritual values and growth that takes place in an individual goes on forever, even into eternity. And I am blessed to be a part of that growth."

* * * * * * *

On June 20 1987, Wycliffe Associates celebrated its twentieth anniversary at a Founder's Banquet held at Westmont College in Santa Barbara, California. Twenty years earlier on a similar June day, Bill Butler had taken a courageous and audacious step of faith when he met Dale Kietzman on the steps of the Wycliffe headquarters building in Santa Ana, California, and said, "I've quit my job, and I've come to work." As the three WA founders—Bill Butler, Dale Kietzman and Rudy Renfer—reminisced about WA's beginnings, Dale said, "When Bill Butler met me that June morning and said he had come to work, that was the precise moment in time when the organization that became known as Wycliffe Associates was born."

All who reminisced about WA's first days and years, and then looked at its growing contribution to Bible translation, concluded that God had indeed performed a miracle. As the evening drew to a close, Elaine Townsend summed up the years. She, like others who had spoken, told about Uncle Cam's desire to involve lay people in the task of Bible translation. After sharing a number of Scripture promises, Elaine concluded with the following story:

Some years ago a two-year-old Canadian

child was lost in a wheat field. All day long and into the night the frantic mother and father and many of their friends and neighbors searched and searched. But no one found the child. Finally one man had an idea. 'I think we will find the child," he said, "if we all join hands and walk in a long, straight line from one end of the field to the other."

And that's what they did, and the child was found.

Said Elaine, "I think this is a vivid example of what we can accomplish when we work together. All of us are needed. No one person possesses all the skills it takes to accomplish the God-given task of Bible translation."

A long time ago another wise person said, "Two are better than one" and "A cord of three strands is not quickly broken" (Ecclesiastes 4:9a, 12b). Indeed, what a difference a team makes!

Postscript

After author Hugh Steven had completed his excellent work on *What a Difference a Team Makes,* he asked me to review the manuscript. It was just at the time the Wycliffe Associates Board was beginning to look for Al Ginty's successor. Hugh's well-researched and well-presented account of the first twenty years of Wycliffe Associates clearly demonstrates how God has raised up specific individuals with specific gifts to lead Wycliffe Associates for specific periods of time, and Al was no exception.

Al has left Wycliffe Associates much stronger than he found it. His gifts of constituent communication, program/ministry development and "bottom-line-results" management have been used by God during this period of WA's growth and consolidation.

As we enter our second twenty years, we have renewed enthusiasm and a clear sense that "the Lord's hand is upon us for good," as Nehemiah said. We know as we continue to approach the future with a servant's heart for supporting the cause of Bible translation through Wycliffe Bible Translators, we can continue to minister meaningfully in the lives of our constituents.

We hope you are edified by Hugh Steven's account of the principles, the "players" and the events the Lord has used to bring Wycliffe Associates to its present position of strength and vigor as the lay affiliate of Wycliffe Bible Translators.

Roger Tompkins
Acting President
January 1, 1988
Santa Ana, California

Martin Huyett

WA's New President

On May 14, 1988, Martin Huyett, former JAARS Executive Director, was unanimously elected by the WA Board to serve as WA's next president.

Martin received his degree in electronics and engineering at John Brown University. His wife Sharon, a registered nurse, was the coordinator for JAARS women's orientation program and is presently working in recruiting at WBT's U.S. Division Office in Huntington Beach, California plus devoting part of her time to a nearby convalescent home. The Huyetts have three children: Anna, 21; John, 20; Charles, 11.

When Bill and Marge Sasnett, members of their home church, left with WBT to serve as Bible translators in Peru, this had a tremendous impact on the Huyetts. As they kept in touch through letters, their interest in Wycliffe eventually led them to join JAARS in 1970 were Martin served as a radio technician.

In 1972, the Lord led the Huyetts to Ghana, West Africa where Martin installed a radio communication network. It was there Martin began to realize that computers, which were not in use at the time, would greatly help to speed the translation process. When the Huyetts returned home two years later and Martin was assigned to head up the JAARS technical orientation program, his interest in computers increased.

In 1976, Martin was asked to direct the radio department, and at that time voiced his vision for the implementation of computers to aid translation work. Two years later he was asked to be WBT's first International Computer Coordinator. As a result, hundreds of translators have reaped the benefits of this time- and money-saving translation tool.

As Martin undertakes the challenge of leading WA, he is ever aware of his need for God's superior wisdom and guidance. James 3:17 and 18 are among his favorite Scriptures: "But the wisdom that comes from heaven is first of all pure; then peace-loving, considerate, submissive, full of mercy and good fruit, impartial and sincere. Peacemakers who sow in peace raise a harvest of righteousness" (NIV).

"I've learned," said Martin, "that God will reveal his will to us as we look to him to be our guide."

Former JAARS Executive Director Martin Huyett assumes leadership as president of Wycliffe Associates. (Dave Duncan photo)

En route to Jungle Camp "Uncle Cam" Townsend (l) chats with a new recruit. (Cornell Capa photo)

An early WA board meeting. Clockwise from left, Dale Kietzman, Douglas Meland, Joseph Profita, William Butler, Wilbur Nelson, Harm Te Velde, James Beam, Paul Robbins and Rey Johnson.

Then WA President Bill Butler (l) discusses plans for WA's new offices with Harold Leasure, building contractor and WA board member.

At groundbreaking for WA's new offices in Orange, California, in May 1971, Dr. Rudolf Renfer (ctr), WA's first president, leads in prayer.

The Auca Rallies introduced thousands of Americans to translator Rachel Saint and Aucas Dawa, Kimo and Uncle Gikito of Ecuador.

Dr. George Cowan, President of Wycliffe Bible Translators, presents an honorary lifetime membership plaque to Dr. Oswald Smith of The Peoples Church of Canada for his help in WA's faith promise banquets and for recording the film, "How God Taught Me to Give."

 The mark of lay involvement is everywhere at Wycliffe Associates. Ollie Carlson finishes the WA emblem and nameplate outside WA's office building in Orange, California.

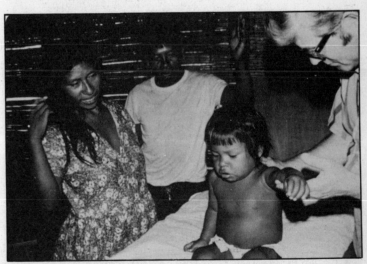

An early emergency—polio among the Aucas in Ecuador—called for immediate attention. Through WA, Physical Therapist E.A. Swanson of Santa Ana, California, learned about the emergency and offered his help.

Boiken visitors from Papua New Guinea with Bettie and Bill Butler at Calvary Church in Santa Ana, California, in October 1971.

Dr. Benjamin Elson (r), WBT's Executive Vice President, thanks Bill Butler for his leadership of WA during its first seven years. Rey Johnson (second from right) became the interim president, assisted by Doug Meland, WA treasurer.

Bob and Beth Bartholomew, WA's first volunteers.

Harry Whitney,
cheerful volunteer
gardener, kept WA's
roses blooming for
several years.

Al Ginty (l), who became WA President in 1981, discusses a building project with John Bender, WA Vice President for Construction.

Dave Crawford, WA Vice President for Personnel and Finance, exchanges information with Personnel Director Linda Hayes (ctr), and Accounting Supervisor Diane Merrell. (Hugh Steven photo)

Mary Cates, Prayer Ministry Director, changes a Watchline tape. Mary, a former WBT member, has been with WA since 1970, serving first as an executive secretary then as editor and director of publications until 1987.
(Hugh Steven photo)

WA Publications Director Mike Yoder (rear) with Design Coordinator John Hamilton and Publications Assistant Lachelle Sevre, selects slides for upcoming publications. (Dave Duncan photo)

Joe Waller, WA Construction Superintendent for the Hillcrest International School, with wife Joy and sons Tim and Ben in Indonesia. (Lonnie Waldner photo)

Ric Winter (r), WA Construction Ministries Director, discusses plans for the Printing Arts Department building with architects at the Wycliffe Center in Dallas, Texas.

Lonnie Waldner (l) WA Construction and Architectural Manager, works on drawings for the Hillcrest International High School in Indonesia with volunteer architect Richard Krantz.

WA Construction Superintendent Sam Moncrieff (second from right) with volunteers from the Dry Creek Bible Church, Dry Creek, Montana, who built a guest house for SIL at Ambon, Maluku Islands, Indonesia. L to r: Tom Langel, LeRoy Ensign, Gregg Mosely, Paul Skinner, Sam Moncrieff, and Andrew Droze.

WA construction volunteers raise a wall for new translation building at Darwin, NT, Australia in 1980. (John Bender photo)

Volunteer telephone specialist Cloyd McCauley tests donated and refurbished telephone equipment being installed at an overseas center.

Volunteer WA well driller Jerry Jameson (l) works with Jay Breazeale at Roberval, Quebec, to provide clean water for seven translation teams. (Dave Beaty photo)

WA Utilities Director Wes Syverson helps to install a new clean water system at an overseas center as part of the water, electrical, telephone (WET) utilities ministry, one of WA's first programs.

*At a WA banquet in Ft. Lauderdale, Florida, Southeast
Area Director Peter Brouillette (l) presents a plaque to
Martha and Roy Long for their faithful, longtime service
as banquet coordinators.*

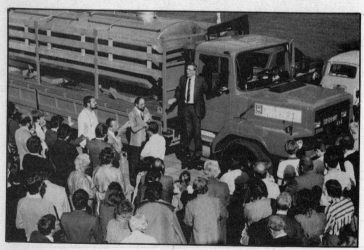

*The new truck WA funded for the translation team in Ghana,
being dedicated at the Tamale Center in 1985.*

Utilities volunteer Clarence Schrader builds an uninterruptible power supply (his own invention) that will keep computer data from being lost in case of a power failure. Clarence is a veteran of many trips overseas to install generators at SIL centers. (Mike Yoder photo)

Roger Petrey (r) former Apollo engineer, has been WA's Mail Room Manager since 1970. Working with him are his wife Barbara (l), volunteer Charlotte Mitchell, and Arthur Carter. (Hugh Steven photo)

Sarah Pease (ctr), WA's first secretary, receives willing help from volunteer Margie Millenaar as Margie's husband Leonard gives WA's front office in Orange, California, a much-needed coat of fresh paint. (Lachelle Sevre photo)

In Dallas, Texas, volunteer Lois Cowles (l), wife of Assistant Construction Superintendent John Cowles, works with helpers Kay Millard and Jane Werkema in the "Boutique." Lois and other volunteers sort, mend, wash, iron, size, and distribute donated clothing to Wycliffe workers and students from all over the world.

WA Lay Involvement Opportunities

When Wycliffe Associates began twenty years ago, they had only three or four service oppourtunities for new Associates. They could form a chapter, go on a trip to Mexico, give money or pray. Today, the possibilities abound. Following is a partial list of current WA lay involvement opportunities:

Banquet Attendee
WA Member
Banquet Coordinator
Construction Volunteer
Work Party Leader
Banquet Reservation Associate
Reading *Newsletter*
Promoting Wycliffe
Hospitality Roster
Construction Superintendent
Recruiting for Volunteers
Banquet Donation
Newsletter Project
Making Faith Promise
Watching or Showing Film
Linen Closet

Property Donor
Banquet Prayer Team
Banquet Publicity
Completing Faith Promise
Wycliffe STA
Dallas Center Volunteer
Recruiting WBT Members
Large Donor
Missions Alive Prayer Team
Tucson Center Volunteer
WA Annual Meeting Attendee
Retirement Housing Board
Huntington Beach Volunteer
Partnership Discovery Participant
Special Event
Missionary Individual Helper
WA Sponsor/500 Club
Banquet Hosts and Greeters
JAARS Center Volunteer
Volunteer Consultant
Prayer Watch Participant
WA Board Member
Extended Skill Volunteer
WA Office Volunteer
Mission Builder for a Church
Providing PDR's and Reference Books
Missionary Financial and/or Prayer Supporter
Donating Equipment
Chapter Member
Reading or Distribution of WA Books

Chapter Leader
Project Prayer Team
Wycliffe Guest Helper
Special Project Donor
Long-Term WA Membership
Wycliffe Lay Rep
Regional Office Volunteer
WA Staff Person
Utilities Equipment Network
WBT Council Member
Banquet Telephone Associate
Aunts and Uncles
Wycliffe Tours
WBT Career Member
Regular WA Donor
Gift Membership
Utility Warehouse
Participation
WBT Regional Advisory Board

For more information, write or call:

Wycliffe Associates
Box 2000
202 S. Prospect Ave.
Orange, CA 92669

(714) 639-9950